WINNING

GOVERNMENT

CONTRACTS

HOW YOUR SMALL BUSINESS CAN FIND AND SECURE FEDERAL GOVERNMENT CONTRACTS UP TO $100,000

MALCOLM PARVEY
DEBORAH ALSTON

CAREER PRESS
HILLSBORO PUBLIC LIBRARIES
Franklin Lakes, NJ
Member of Washington County
COOPERATIVE LIBRARY SERVICES

WINNING GOVERNMENT CONTRACTS
EDITED BY KATE HENCHES
TYPESET BY MICHAEL FITZGIBBON
Cover design by Rob Johnson/Johnson Design
Printed in the U.S.A. by Book-mart Press
GSA Advantage!® is a registered trademark.

To order this title, please call toll-free 1-800-CAREER-1 (NJ and
Canada: 201-848-0310) to order using VISA or MasterCard, or for further
information on books from Career Press.

The Career Press, Inc., 3 Tice Road, PO Box 687,
Franklin Lakes, NJ 07417
www.careerpress.com

Library of Congress Cataloging-in-Publication Data
Parvey, Malcolm.
    Winning government contracts : how your small business can
find and and secure federal government contracts up to $100,000 / by
Malcolm Parvey & Deborah Alston.
       p. cm.
    Includes index.
    ISBN-13: 978-1-56414-975-6
    ISBN-10: 1-56414-975-7
                  1. Public contracts—United States. I. Alston, Deborah.
II. Title.
       39789515   3/09
    HD3861.U6P36 2008
    346.7302'3—dc22

                                                              2007035255

"This small business guide provides a concise and clear path for anyone seeking to participate in capitalizing on the opportunities of the federal marketplace. The guide is skillfully organized to simplify the intimidating federal maze of contracting jargon and regulations. Even as a former government employee with over 20 years' experience in contracting for services and construction, this handbook provides me invaluable guidance. Today, as an inexperienced small business entrepreneur seeking federal contract awards, this is my first resource of choice concerning federal contracting opportunities."

Thomas J. Marks Jr., Col. (Ret) P.E.
V.P. Federal Services
FacilityOne

"During the last three years Mr. Parvey has been instrumental in assisting Admiral Metals in securing more then 300 Federal Government Contracts. His 30 years of experience has really paid off for us."

Michael Thomas
Government Contracts Administrator

"With Mr. Parvey's guidance, Minutemen Trucks has secured federal government contracts in the last year that exceeds 10 percent of our previous years' gross sales. Not only is the federal government one of our biggest customers, it is also one of our best paying customers."

William Witcher
Partner
Minuteman Trucks, Inc.

ACKNOWLEDGMENTS

I am so happy to have this opportunity to publicly acknowledge all the federal government employees with whom I have had the pleasure of working throughout my 30-year career. I have never encountered an organization that was so helpful, so dedicated, or so professional than the procurement sectors of all the federal agencies. I cannot say enough good things about the vast majority of these individuals. My experience with them has always been positive. These are hard-working, well-trained professionals who are always willing to help small businesses whenever possible.

CONTENTS

Introduction   **13**

How to Use This Book   **23**

Chapter 1: Introduction to Federal Government Sales   **27**

Are You a "Small Business"? Determining Size Standards

Resources for Small Businesses

· The Small Business Administration

· Women-Biz.Gov

· Small Business Administration's Free Online Government Contracts Training

· Small Business Administration Subcontracting Network

· Procurement Technical Assistance Centers (PTAC)

· SBA Agency Procurement Forecasts

How the Federal Government Buys What It Needs

· Invitation for Bid (IFB)

· Request for Proposal (RFP)

· Request for Quotation (RFQ)

· Best Value Purchasing

· Consolidated Purchasing Programs

· Government Credit Card Purchases

· Online Reverse Auctions—FedBid

Important Business Codes and Numbers

· Data Universal Numbering System (DUNS)

· Tax Identification Number (TIN)

· Central Contractor Registration (CCR)

· Trading Partners Identification Number (TPIN)

· Marketing Partners Identification Number (MPIN)

· Commercial and Government Entity (CAGE) Codes

· North American Industrial Classification System (NAICS)

· Standard Industrial Classification (SIC) Codes

- Federal Supply Classification Codes (FSC)
- Online Representations and Certifications (ORCA)

A Checklist for You

Chapter 2: Searching the Federal Business Opportunities (FedBizOpps) Website   **47**

The Federal Business Opportunities Website
- The Federal Business Opportunities (FedBizOpps) Homepage
- Searching the Site
- Methods of Searching

Start Search—Click Here to Begin Your Search.
- Interpreting the Search Results
- Understanding the Synopsis
- General Information
- Contracting Office Address
- Approved Sources
- Other Mandatory or Preferred Sources
- Solicitations With Drawings or Specifications
- The Automated Best Value System (ABVS)

Additional Information

Point of Contact
- Numbered Notes
- Register to Receive Notification
- Understanding Amendments and Modifications
- The Site Visit
- Questions and Answers
- The Solicitation Package

The Set-Aside Programs
- Small Business Concern
- Very Small Business Concern
- Woman-Owned Business Concern
- Small Disadvantaged 8(a) Businesses
- Minority-Owned and Small Minority-Owned Businesses
- HUB-Zone Businesses
- Veteran-Owned and Service-Disabled Veteran-Owned Businesses

Other Important Programs
- Sole Source
- Qualified Products List (QPL)
- Qualified Suppliers List for Manufacturers (QSLM) and Distributors (QSLD)

     · Other Government Agency Standards
     · Federal Acquisition Regulations (FAR)
     · The Contracting Officer
  Related Links
     · Business Partner Network
     · Federal Agency Business Forecasts
     · Federal Assets Sales
     · Federal Grants
     · USAGov
     · Minority Business Development Agency
     · SUB-Net
     · Integrated Acquisition Environment (IAE)
     · FedTeds
     · Vendor Notification Service
     · Section 508
     · Hurricane and Disaster Response Contracting
     · FedBizOpps Homepage—Vendor Link
  A Word on Acronymns

Chapter 3: Searching and Quoting in the Defense Logistics Agency's Internet Bid Board System (DIBBS) Website   **93**
  The DIBBS Homepage
     · The Vendor Tab
     · The Solicitations Tab
     · RFP/IFB Database
     · Other DLA Opportunities
  Understanding the Solicitation Numbering System
  Automated Awards—PACE
  Manual Awards
  Auto-IDPOs
  Approved Part Numbers and Alternate Part Numbers
  The References Tab
  NSN/FSC Query Database
  All FSCs Managed by DLA
  Master Solicitation Document
  The Automated Best Value System
  The Technical Data Tab
  Drawings and Technical Documents
     · Viewing Drawings

· Still Can't Find What You Are Looking For?

Other Websites for Obtaining Drawings

Procurement History

Other Important Programs

   · The Quality Shelf Life Program

   · Environmental "Green" Purchasing Programs

   · Approved Environmental Attributes

Other "Green" Programs

Quoting in DIBBS

   · Step-by-Step Through Your Online Quote in DIBBS

   · Batch Quoting

Finding Information on Awards

Icons Used in DIBBS

Chapter 4: Additional Procurement Sites   **117**

Procurement Gateway (ProGate)

   · Your Search Options at This Site

   · The Search Results

   · How to Obtain Drawings

   · Where to Obtain Specifications and Standards

   · Creating a Custom Procurement Gateway Profile

   · Army Single Face to Industry (ASFI)

The United States Postal Service

The Veterans Administration

Federal Prison Industries (UNICOR)

   · Federal Bureau of Prisons

United States Patent Office

Sub-Contracting Opportunities—SubNet

The Government Printing Office

Market Information at the Federal Procurement Data Center

Additional Procurement Sites

   · A Sampling of Other Procurement Sites

Chapter 5: Submitting Your Hard Copy Offer

Using Federal Standard Forms (SF18, SF1449, SF33)   **135**

The Uniform Contract Format

Section A: Solicitation/Contract Form

Section B: Supplies/Services and Prices/Costs

Section C: Description/Specifications/Work Statement

Section D: Packaging and Marking

Sections E and F: Inspection and Acceptance, and Deliveries or Performance

Section G: Contract Administration Data
Section H: Special Contract Requirements
Section I: Contract Clauses
· Instructions to Offerors
· Offeror Representations and Certifications
· Acknowledgment of Solicitations Amendments
· Past Performance Information
· Changes to Contract Terms and Conditions
· For How Long Will the Price You Give Be Valid?
· Samples
· Late Submissions, Modifications, Revisions and Withdrawals of Offers
· Contract Award
· Multiple Awards
· Specifications and Standards
· Evaluation
· Contract Terms and Conditions
· Contract Terms and Conditions Required to Implement Statutes or Executive Orders
· More Cited Regulations
Section J: List of Attachments
Section K: Representations, Certifications, and Other Statements
Section L: Instructions, Conditions, and Notices
· Possible Clauses
Section M: Evaluation Factors
Combined Synopsis/Solicitations
Submitting Your Offer
Chapter 6: Service Contracts   165
Part One—The Price Proposal
Part Two—The Technical Proposal
Part Three—Past Performance Information
Wage Determinations
Contractor Manpower Reporting
Insurance
Site Visit
Federal Travel Regulations
Evaluating Your Offer
A-76 Standard Streamlined Competitions
More Resources

Chapter 7: Fulfilling the Terms of Your Contract   179

Packing and Marking Requirements
- Liability for Damage Caused by Inadequate Packaging
- Unique Identification of Items— Bar Codes and RFID Tags
- Bar Codes
- Radio Frequency Identification (RFID) Tags
- Wood Packaging Material
- More Information

Shipping Your Product
- DD250: The Distribution Data Report

Inspection and Acceptance
- Inspection
- Acceptance

Invoicing
- Web Invoicing System (WINS)
- Wide Area Workflow
- Getting Started
- Submitting Invoices
- Wide Area Workflow Training
- Using Wide Area Workflow for Vendors—A Student Guide
- Practice Sites

The Post-Award Orientation Conference

Contract Performance Monitoring

Reporting

Breach of Contract

Performance Reports

Veterans Reporting Requirements

Chapter 8: Stepping Up to the Next Level   193

Government Wide Acquisition Contracts for Information Technology

The General Services Administration's (GSA) Federal Supply Schedule

Other Government Wide Acquisition Contracts

In Conclusion

Appendix   199

Central Contractor Registration Worksheet

Offeror's Representations and Certifications Applications Worksheet

U.S. Trade Agreements Act, Designated Countries

Unit of Issue Codes

Index   229

About the Author   235

INTRODUCTION

SELLING TO THE FEDERAL GOVERNMENT: A GUIDE FOR SMALL BUSINESSES

There were approximately 22.9 million small businesses in the United States in 2002. Small businesses provide approximately 75 percent of the net new jobs added to the economy; they represent 99.7 percent of all employers; they employ more than 50 percent of the private workforce; they provide for more than 40 percent of private sales in the country; and they account for more than 39 percent of jobs in the high technology field.

Federal regulations state that if any government agency is going to make a purchase estimated to be $100,000 or less, it *must* be set aside for small businesses. Federal agencies must set up contracting goals—for example, that 23 percent of all government purchases should be from small businesses. Federal agencies have a statutory obligation to reach out to small businesses and to purchase from them whenever possible.

My name is Malcolm Parvey. I am an independent Sales and Marketing Consultant with more than 30 years of experience assisting companies in securing federal government contracts. Through the years, I have completed hundreds of offers just like those you will find in this book.

I decided to write this book because I could never find any information that would show a step-by-step procedure to finding, understanding, and submitting government competitive bids up to $100,000. It is my understanding that there is no book, agency, or school that teaches you a step-by-step method of how to find sales opportunities, submit offers, receive awards, and ensure prompt payment for government contracts up to $100,000.

In my client-based business, it is my responsibility to perform all administrative functions prior to award, other than determining the price. This includes, but is not limited to, the following basic tasks:

- Searching federal government procurement sites on a daily basis to find appropriate opportunities for my clients.

- Researching the sales opportunities in order to acquire drawings, specifications, samples, past procurement history, and any other pertinent information that is available.

- Completing the bid package.

- Submitting it to the proper agency, in my client's name.

- Tracking the results of the offers and informing my client of which companies submitted offers, and their prices; which company was awarded the contract; and the awarded price. When my client is awarded the contract I track all invoices to ensure prompt payment.

I wrote this book along with my co-author, Deborah Alston. To begin with Deborah did not know much about this market, just like you! It was her rule that if she could not understand what I was talking about, then no one else would!

Deborah and I set out to try to explain government contracting to the beginner. The book is written in simple language, without using government jargon where it was at all possible. We address the common issues of small companies that would like to get into this market but don't know where to begin. The book's simple, step-by-step writing fashion ensures that anyone who would like to explore this exciting business opportunity can quickly learn enough to find out if they are competitive.

If you would like more information about the services I provide, visit my Website at *www.sell2gov.com.*

Because of my years of experience assisting many different types of industries, I feel more than qualified to explain to the small-business community the mechanics of finding sales opportunities in the federal government marketplace, submitting competitive bids, and ensuring prompt payment.

This book has been written so that you will have a clear understanding, in layman's terms, of how the federal government marketplace operates. This book will also give you a detailed step-by-step guide to finding and submitting offers, receiving contracts, and getting paid on time. In my experience, the federal government is by far the biggest and best customer in the entire world for small businesses! The subjects that are going to be discussed in this book refer to the small business set-aside program.

Once you have finished reading this book, you should be able to go to your computer and start the procedure of submitting competitive offers. You should also be able to refer back to this book for any guidance you may need.

A NOTE ON LINK INFORMATION

Throughout this book, you will come across many links to Websites. Some links are to government sites; others are organization sites or commercial sites. These links allow you to follow up on the information I have provided, or to find more detailed information on a particular topic that may be of interest to you.

Although every effort has been made to keep the link information in this book current, we are aware that any links we provide can quickly become obsolete.

As an extra service to our readers, and to ensure that this book remains as up-to-date as possible, we will be providing updated link information on my company Website at *www.sell2gov.com* and at *www.sell2gov.com/updated_links.htm*.

We also welcome your input! If you find that a link has changed, please let us know via the "Contact Us" section of the Website. We will do everything we can to ensure that these links remain an invaluable source of information.

THE 25 BIGGEST MISCONCEPTIONS SMALL BUSINESSES HAVE REGARDING FEDERAL CONTRACTING

1. I am too small to do business with the federal government.

The federal government's goal is to set aside 23 percent of their purchases specifically for small businesses. Each agency must do their very best to meet that goal. If you can supply the product in the volume and time frame required, you are not too small. There are many daily sales opportunities for $10,000 or less.

2. I don't have time to learn about this.

How much time do you currently spend on your most favored customers? Remember: The federal government is the biggest customer in the entire world! This one customer can give you more business than all of your commercial customers combined! This book will take you step-by-step through the entire process—from finding the sales opportunities, putting in a bid, and following through after you are awarded. Much of the paperwork is exactly the same from bid to bid, so that once you have prepared a few offers you will feel much more confident. Once you are familiar with the format of a particular agency's site, you will find that you can submit many electronic bids in as little as six minutes!

3. You need contacts in the federal government to win an award.

No! You just need to know where the sales opportunities are. The federal government issues more than 10,000 different sales opportunities every day, and many are issued and awarded automatically by computer.

4. I can't make a profit in this marketplace.

You will never know whether or not you are competitive in this marketplace unless you get involved! Using this book you will be able to find out what the government is paying for an item right now, *before* you put in your bid! Also, remember that the purchase may be set-aside exclusively for small, woman-owned, minority-owned, veteran-owned, or disadvantaged businesses. This book will show you how to identify if you qualify for these set-asides. Another factor to remember is that, often, the contract will be awarded using what is known as Best Value Purchasing rather than simply on price alone—if you can offer a better delivery time, or a better warranty than your competitors you *will* be awarded the contract, even if your price is somewhat higher!

5. I tried this before, but it didn't work out.

Plenty has changed in the last few years—what used to take 10 days to complete, now thanks to the internet, takes only 10 minutes! The e-government initiative has made it much simpler to find bids and submit offers, particularly for purchases less than $100,000—known as the Simplified Acquisition Threshold.

6. My small business can't handle multimillion-dollar contracts.

There are many smaller bid opportunities out there for you—you just need to know how to find them! This book shows you where they are! There are an estimated 10,000 sales opportunities each day, across all agencies—95 percent of them are estimated to be $100,000 or less!

7. I don't understand the jargon.

This book explains each government term in simple easy-to-understand language that does not assume any previous knowledge in this area.

8. I don't know where to begin.

The first step will be to register your company at the Central Contractor Registration site. You must be registered at this site in order to receive an award. In Chapter 1, we take you step-by-step through the registration process. We also explain the other important business codes and numbers you will need in order to begin.

9. I am a small service company—there's no market for me.

Are you a small landscaping company? The government contracts for lawn mowing and grounds maintenance. Are you a staffing agency? The government contracts out much of their administrative work to civilian contractors. Are you a small building company? There are many opportunities for you out there—you just need to know where to find them! Are you a small marketing/public relations firm? A video production firm? An online distance-learning company? A computer programming firm? I have helped *all* these service companies to win government contracts in the 30 years he has been in this business, and this book can help your company too!

10. The government takes too long to pay.

The federal government is required by regulations to pay small businesses in 30 days. You need to understand their invoicing system. Many awards are paid via Electronic Funds Transfer, and new systems such as Wide Area Workflow allow you to keep track of your invoice as it travels through the system until you are paid. This book shows you how to get started using these systems.

11. I don't have a GSA contract, so I can't submit competitive bids.

The *only* requirement for you to be awarded a government contract (and to get paid) is to be registered in the Central Contractors Registration (CCR) site. GSA contracts are just one of the many tools the government uses to make purchases, and we discuss the advantages of getting your GSA contract number in this book. But you do *not* need one in order to begin. If you find out that you are competitive and you can win awards, then a GSA contract will be another tool for you.

12. There is too much competition in this marketplace.

Fewer than 2 percent of registered U.S. companies actively seek out this market. This could mean that fewer than 2 percent of your competitors actively seek out this market. This book will show you how to do some research to find out who your competitors are in this market.

13. I sell products that are made outside of the United States.

The Buy American Act places certain restrictions on foreign products but there are more than a dozen exceptions to this regulation. For example, if at least 51 percent of the cost of producing the finished item is incurred in the United States, Mexico, or Canada, it is *not* considered an imported item. Use this book to find out more.

14. There are too many rules and regulations.

Federal agencies are strongly encouraged to make use of accepted commercial standards whenever possible, so this need not be an obstacle.

15. There isn't anyone to go to for direction.

Take advantage of local organizations that can help you get started—for example the Small Business Administration (SBA), or the local Procurement Technical Assistance Centers (PTAC). Information on how to locate your nearest office is located in Chapter 1.

16. I need Drawings and Specifications for my products.

This book will show you step-by-step where to go, and how to download drawings and specifications immediately from the Internet.

17. I am a dealer—I won't be able to sell to the government.

If you are a dealer, you can still sell your products to the government. This book shows you how.

18. I'll just hand this one over to Bob! (or Barbara!)

Don't try to give the responsibility for this to someone who already has too much to do, because it won't get done! Assign someone in the company to research this thoroughly so that you give it a fair shot. It doesn't need to be one of your executive staff, but someone in the company should read this book, find out who your competition is, do some research into the market, put in some bids, and follow up on them. If one agency doesn't buy your products, look elsewhere. This is the *only* way to really tell if this market is right for your company. You will never know until you try!

19. I'll just skim over the details—there is too much to read.

Like any other sales opportunity you must understand the terms and conditions of the contract before you put in your offer. Everything is there in black and white, and a few moments checking out the details could save you a lot of time later on. If you have a question on a bid there is always a point of contact on the very first page to answer all and any questions.

20. I need professional training—it will cost too much, and take too much time.

Look at this book as your training manual. Everything you need to know in order to win contracts is in the book. In addition, there are many free training seminars available at your local Small Business Administration (SBA) office, or the local Procurement Technical Assistance Center (PTAC). There are a number of free online government training resources that will help you to master any of the systems you need to understand. For example, the new Wide Area Work Flow (WAWF) system, which tracks products and services from delivery to invoicing and payment, has a free online training session to help you navigate the system, as well as a practice site where you can fill out dummy invoices to understand how the system works. Remember that government officers are always willing to help you with any problems—you just have to ask!

21. The agency will never return my calls.

The agency's Contracting Officer really is there to help you! Send an e-mail to the point of contact listed in the solicitation and you will get a reply—these people really are professional, highly trained, courteous, and patient.

22. I already do business with a federal agency.

Just because you have done business with the United States Postal Service, the Air Force, or the Secret Service does not mean you know how to do business with other agencies! Every agency does business differently, but they are all required to use the same basic regulations. In the commercial marketplace, you know that every sale is different, even though you are selling the same product or service, and you must tailor your approach accordingly. In a similar way each agency is different because they all have a different mission.

23. I don't need to keep records.

Wrong! The government never throws away records, and neither should you! Keep a record of every sales opportunity with which you are involved. If you speak to someone on the phone, send an e-mail to follow up. When you win a contract keep every record for a minimum of three years after the contract has expired.

24. My record with one agency won't help me get business with other agencies.

You think that being a good vendor only counts with the particular purchasing agent with which you did business? The government keeps a report card in a central location for each vendor so that other purchasing agents can see how well you performed on previous contracts. Your good record counts!

25. I'll look at this next week—or next month....

The opportunities for your small business *are* out there! Don't wait for some vague time in the future when you think you will be able to find the time! Find the time *today* and *get started now*!

How to Use This Book

There are many different federal government agencies, with different responsibilities and mandates, but they all need to purchase goods and services. Many agencies use their own Websites to advertise sales opportunities, and in many instances you may submit an offer electronically through the site.

It would be almost impossible to cover every agency's site individually, because there are so many of them. Instead, we have chosen several important sites to look at in detail. Once you are familiar with the way these specific sites advertise their sales opportunities and accept your offers, you will be confident enough to find your way around most other federal agency sites.

In Chapter 1, you will find an overview of how the federal government purchases the products and services it needs; an explanation of how the Small Business Administration determines size standards; and a comprehensive list of the business codes and numbers you will need to obtain in order to begin selling to the federal government, exactly where to go to get them, and why they are important.

In Chapter 2, we look in detail at the Federal Business Opportunities Website, or FedBizOpps. This is the central site where most agencies must post their sales opportunities if they are estimated to be valued at more than $25,000. The initial notice is posted in FedBizOpps, and a link will take you to the specific agency's site for the details of the bid.

Chapter 3 looks closely at the Department of Defense's Website, known as DIBBS (Defense Internet Bid Board System). The sales opportunities at this site can be for as little as $50, and can reach to as high as several million dollars or more. (Remember that sales opportunities posted in DIBBS that are valued at more than $25,000 will ALSO be posted in FedBizOpps.)

In many instances you will be able to submit your bids electronically, so we also take you step-by-step through the electronic bidding process at DIBBS. Whereas other sites may have their specific electronic bid processes, once you have seen exactly how the system works at DIBBS, you will be able to use that knowledge if you wish to bid electronically at other agency sites in the future.

Chapter 4 takes a look at some of the many other government sites you may wish to search, including the Army Single Face to Industry, Procurement Gateway, and others.

Chapter 5 takes you step-by-step through a hard copy or paper offer. Though there are many opportunities for you to submit your bids electronically (see electronic bidding at DIBBS in Chapter 3), at other times the bid package must be filled in and mailed or faxed in a hard copy, or paper format. Once you have read Chapter 5 you will become more familiar with the way this process works.

Chapter 6 discusses some additional information that is important for you to know if you are a company that provides a service—for example, if you are a construction company, a landscaping firm, a public relations business, and so on.

Chapter 7 looks at what happens once you have been awarded the contract. This chapter covers such important points as commercial versus military packaging, RFID and barcodes regulations, shipping requirements, inspection and acceptance policies, and invoicing, including Wide Area Workflow procedures.

Chapter 8 discusses the additional opportunities that are available to you with long-term, multi-year contracts, such as the General Service Administration's (GSA) Federal Supply Schedule contract, and government-wide contracts.

The Appendix contains useful worksheets and tables of information.

A WORD ON ACRONYMS

There are many acronyms used throughout the federal contracting arena. For further clarification you may wish to use these Websites. If in doubt, ask the Contracting Officer!

Defense Acquisition University: Defense Acquisition Acronyms and Terms

www.dau.mil/pubs/glossary/preface.asp

Defense Supply Center Columbus Acronyms

www.dscc.dla.mil/search/acronym/default.asp

A WORD ON SOME NECESSARY EVILS

This book is intended as a working manual, something you can refer to regularly as you begin to search the various agency sites for sales opportunities. For that reason there are occasions in the book where information is repeated from one chapter to another, rather than simply referring you to a particular section of the book; that way all the information is right where you need it. For example, any federal contract valued at $25,000 or greater is listed at FedBizOpps, but the same notice may also appear at the purchasing agency's particular site.

CHAPTER I

INTRODUCTION TO FEDERAL GOVERNMENT SALES

AN OVERVIEW

Are you a small business? In this introductory section we begin by examining exactly how the government determines whether you are considered a small business, and how you can find out whether you are eligible to be considered as a small business.

Resources. This is followed by information on the many organizations that can give you advice and assistance on doing business with the federal government, such as the Small Business Administration (SBA) and the government's Procurement Technical Assistance Centers (PTAC).

How the federal government buys what it needs. This section gives you a brief overview of exactly how the federal government buys the things it needs, and explains such terms as Invitation for Bid, Request for Proposal, Request for Quote, and Best Value Purchasing. We briefly examine the many government Consolidated Purchase programs that are available, such as Multi-Agency Contracts (MACs), Government-Wide Acquisition Contracts (GWACs) and General Services Administration (GSA) Schedule contracts. In addition, we look at the increasing use of the government Purchase Cards (credit cards).

Important codes and numbers: You will need to obtain these in order to begin selling to the federal government. Each term is explained in plain language so that you understand why it is important to know these numbers, where you can find them, and so on. We take you step-by-step though each number or code, and explain clearly where to go to obtain each one. In addition, we take you step-by-step through the Central Contractors Registration (CCR) site, and the new Online Representations and Certifications Applications (ORCA) site, where you must register your company in order to do business with the federal government.

ARE YOU A SMALL BUSINESS? DETERMINING SIZE STANDARDS

Obviously if you wish to take advantage of the various programs that are set-aside for small businesses, you must first determine if you are eligible.

A small business is one that:

- Is Organized for Profit.
- Operates in the United States.
- Pays taxes, and uses American products, labor, and materials.
- Does not exceed the size standard for its industry.

The Small Business Administration uses the North American Industrial Classification System (NAICS) to determine the types of industries and their size standards. Size standards are usually stated in terms either of the number of employees in a company, or the company's average annual receipts. For a products company the size standard is determined by your annual average receipts; for a service company the size standard is determined by the number of employees (including both full- and part-time).

In the chart that follows, a business in one of the industry groups on the left is considered to be a Small Business if its size is not greater than the standard on the right:

Industry Group	Size Standard
Manufacturing	500 employees
Wholesale Trade	100 employees
Agriculture	$750,000
Retail Trade	$6.5 million
General and Heavy Construction	$31 million
Dredging	$18.5 million
Special Trade Contractors	$13 million
Travel Agencies	$3.5 million
Business and Personal Services	$6.5 million
Architectural, Engineering, Surveying and Mapping Services	$4.5 million
Dry Cleaning, Carpet Cleaning Services	$4.5 million

You may wish to research size standards in more detail on the Small Business Administration's Website: *www.sba.gov/size.*

RESOURCES FOR SMALL BUSINESSES

There are many government agencies that can help you. These links are all good places to begin:

The Small Business Administration

http://www.sba.gov/

WomenBiz.Gov

www.womenbiz.gov

Small Business Administration's Free Online Government Contracts Training

http://www.sba.gov/services/training/onlinecourses/training_atc_sbtc.html

Small Business Administration Subcontracting Network

http://web.sba.gov/subnet/

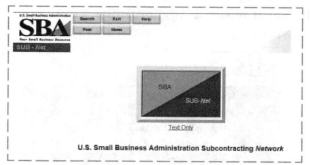

Procurement Technical Assistance Centers (PTAC)

http://www.dla.mil/db/procurem.htm

Administered by the Department of Defense, these centers offer local, low-cost assistance to companies wishing to market their products and services to federal, state, and local governments.

DEPARTMENT OF DEFENSE

Procurement Technical Assistance Centers

The Defense Logistics Agency, on behalf of the Secretary of Defense, administers the DoD Procurement Technical Assistance Program (PTAP). PTA Centers are a local resource available at no or nominal cost that can provide assistance to business firms in marketing products and services to the Federal, state and local governments.

SBA Agency Procurement Forecasts

http://www.acqnet.gov/comp/procurement_forecasts/index.html

Acquisition Central

acquisition.gov

Agency Recurring Procurement Forecasts:

HOME PAGE — Select an Agency

SMALL BUSINESS INFORMATION — Select an Agency

BUSINESS OPPORTUNITIES — Select an Agency

PROCUREMENT FORECAST — Select an Agency

HOW THE FEDERAL GOVERNMENT BUYS WHAT IT NEEDS

In 1994, the government enacted the Federal Acquisition Streamlining Act, which simplified the way in which government purchases under $100,000 are made. In addition, all federal purchases more than $2,500 but less than $100,000 must now be set aside exclusively for small businesses.

Government purchases of $2,500 or less are now classified as "micro-purchases" and can be made without obtaining competitive quotes. These purchases can be made using a government Purchase Card, and are no longer reserved exclusively for small businesses.

INVITATION FOR BID (IFB)

When the government agency has a clear and complete picture of their needs, they will issue an Invitation for Bid (IFB). The IFB contains an exact description of the product or service, instructions for preparing a bid, the conditions for purchase, packaging, delivery, shipping and payment, contract clauses to be included, and the deadline for submitting bids. On the stated Bid Opening Date and Time, each sealed bid is opened in public at the purchasing office. All the bids are read aloud and recorded, and a contract is awarded.

REQUEST FOR PROPOSAL (RFP)

When the value of the contract exceeds $100,000 and the product or service is considered to be highly technical in nature, the government may issue a Request for Proposal (RFP). In this case the agency will describe the product or service that it needs, and solicit proposals from prospective contractors on how they intend to carry out that request, and at what price. Proposals in response to an RFP can be subject to negotiation after they have been submitted.

REQUEST FOR QUOTATION (RFQ)

Sometimes the government is simply looking at the possibility of acquiring a product or service. In this case it will issue a Request for Quotation (RFQ). A response to an RFQ is not considered to be an offer, and does not form a binding contract. The RFQ is an offer by the government to the supplier to buy certain supplies or services upon specified terms and conditions. A contract is only established after a supplier accepts the offer.

If the agency estimates that the award will exceed $25,000 then it must be synopsized on the Federal Business Opportunities Website, FedBizOpps. If the agency estimates that the award will not exceed $100,000 then it will be set-aside for certain categories of businesses.

The FedBizOpps Website is *www.fbo.gov*.

BEST VALUE PURCHASING

One of the most significant changes to be aware of is the increased importance of "Best Value" purchasing. Instead of making an award based solely on price, the government can now consider awarding a contract to a higher priced offer, if they can determine that it best satisfies their needs. For example, a higher priced offer may have a better warranty or a faster delivery date. If the purchase is going to be awarded under the "Best Value" criteria, it will state this in the solicitation document, and will include a description of the evaluation criteria, award factors, and factors other than the price that will be considered in making a contract award.

CONSOLIDATED PURCHASING PROGRAMS

Many agencies have common purchasing needs—for example, carpeting, furniture, office supplies, maintenance, or perishable foods. In many cases the government can realize economies of scale by centralizing the purchasing of these types of products or services. Multi-Agency Contracts (MACs) and Government-Wide Acquisition Contracts (GWACs) are important programs and their use has greatly increased over the last few years.

General Services Administration (GSA) Schedule contracts are also being used more extensively. Government buyers can quickly fill their requirements by issuing orders against existing contracts without going out on competitive bid. Agencies can also award several contracts to different firms for the same products and services. Obtaining a GSA Schedule contract number allows your company to be exposed to this marketplace. Your products and services will be posted onto a government Website, so that buyers can obtain information on the products it needs without going out on competitive bid.

For more information, go to the GSA Website: *www.gsa.gov.*

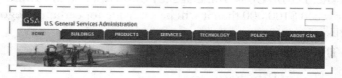

GOVERNMENT CREDIT CARD PURCHASES

In fiscal year 2002, government credit card holders purchased more than 6 billion worth of goods and services. According to the General Accounting Office (GAO), there are 720,000 federal government employees with credit cards. Their credit limits vary from $20,000 to $1,000,000 per year, depending on their position within the agency.

For purchases under $250, there is no requirement for a competitive price. These purchases can be made with any business, either inside or outside the government marketplace.

For purchases ranging from $251 to $2,500, the credit card holder must attempt to secure a minimum of three competitive verbal quotes from approved vendors.

These government credit card holders have a minimum order limitation of $2,500 and a minimum annual credit limit of $20,000.

ONLINE REVERSE AUCTIONS — FEDBID

More and more bids are being issued using the online competitive reverse auction service, called FedBid, Inc. More than 17 government agencies already use this service.

FedBid, Inc., states that in 2005, 70 percent of the dollars that were awarded through their site went to Small Businesses.

Federal buyers may set purchase parameters at the site: they can request bids only from small, woman-owned, or veteran-owned businesses, or they may prefer or require participants to be GSA contract holders. The buyers describe exactly the items they wish to purchase and the quantity required, list any special instructions (requiring new items only for example), and specify shipping and delivery details.

More than 1,000 procurement professionals at dozens of federal organizations use FedBid to procure hundreds of millions of dollars worth of commodities and simple services.

A specific time period for bids is issued, and during this time period you may submit a series of price quotes, which descend in price. This type of reverse auction is becoming popular for agencies where the items they wish to purchase are commercial off-the-shelf (COTS) items, with specific requirements for a particular manufacturer and part number, and price is the major factor in determining an award.

The bids are accepted at the online exchange site: *www.FedBid.com.*

There is no cost to register, review procurement data, or make an offer.

The company takes a small fee from the winning vendor.

More than 45 percent of sales are for Information Technology equipment (printers, servers, monitors, and so forth) and more than half the sales are closed via General Service Administration (GSA) Schedule contracts.

Once you have registered at the site, you may view the opportunities that are available for you to bid. You will be able to see a description of the items required, along with any restrictions or special instructions, as well as the name of the agency involved, and the ending time for bids. In addition, you are able to track the status of any existing bids you have placed and the results of bids once they have been awarded.

Important Business Codes and Numbers

In order to begin selling to the federal government, you must first register your business at certain government sites, and you will also need to know several important business codes or numbers. You may already have some of these numbers and codes. They are all easy to get from the appropriate agency.

To begin, you will need to know your company's Dun & Bradstreet number (DUNS number) and your Tax Identification Number (TIN number).

Data Universal Numbering System (DUNS)

This number is used by federal agencies to certify that you are financially capable of fulfilling your obligations. This number is available at no cost to you from the commercial company Dun & Bradstreet.

You must have a different DUNS number for each physical location or different address in your company as well as each legal division that may be co-located.

You may access the company Website for more information, or you may call them at 1–866–705–5711.

Website address:

http://ccr.dnb.com/ccr/pages/CCRSearch.jsp

TAX IDENTIFICATION NUMBER (TIN)

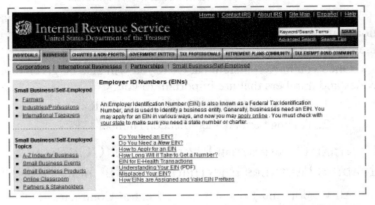

This number allows any federal agency to certify the type of organization submitting an offer (Incorporated, Sole Proprietor, and so on). Your Tax Identification Number (TIN) is a nine-digit number, which can be from one of two sources:

1. Your Employer Identification Number (EIN) assigned by the IRS (*http://www.irs.gov/ businesses/small/article/0,,id=98350,00.html*).

2. Your Social Security Number (SSN) assigned by the Social Security Administration (SSA) (*http:/ www.ssa.gov/replace_sscard.html*).

In order to complete the mandatory registration at the Central Contractors Registration (CCR) site, and qualify as a vendor eligible to bid for federal government contracts, the Tax Identification Number (TIN) and the Taxpayer Name combination you provide in the CCR must match *exactly* to the TIN and Taxpayer Name used in federal tax matters.

 Note that from October 30, 2005, all TINs will be validated by the Inland Revenue Service (IRS). You will not be allowed to have an active CCR registration without a validated TIN. The TIN matching process is a joint effort between the General Services Administration (GSA), the Department of Defense (DOD), and the Inland Revenue Service (IRS) to improve the quality of data in government acquisition systems.

Once you have your DUNS Number and your Tax Identification Number, you are ready to begin your company registration at the CCR site.

Once you have registered at CCR you will also be given other codes and numbers that are important to you:

1. Central Contractor Registration (CCR).
2. Trading Partners Identification Number (TPIN).

CENTRAL CONTRACTOR REGISTRATION (CCR) AND TRADING PARTNERS IDENTIFICATION NUMBER (TPIN)

All vendors must register at the Central Contractor Registration (CCR) site in order to be awarded government contracts. You must provide basic information about your company in order to register. This information is used to confirm your company status, and also allows future payments to be made via electronic funds transfers. The information you provide will be shared with authorized federal government offices.

CCR Website: *www.ccr.gov*

Click on the tab at the top of the screen called "Handbook" to download the complete CCR handbook, which takes you through the registration process page-by-page.

Hover over the tab called "Vendor Corner" and you will see information on how the registration process works.

Click on "Register in CCR" to begin. You must have your company's Dun & Bradstreet number (DUNS number) available at this point.

If you cannot complete the registration in a single session, you may save the partial data and resume the process at another time. To do this, click "Save/Validate Data" and make a note of the temporary code that you are given. This code, along with your DUNS number, will allow you to pick up the registration where you left off, when you return to it at a later date. You can easily see which information is incomplete by viewing the "Show Errors" section of the screen.

Once your registration is completed and submitted, you will be issued a Trading Partners Identification Number (TPIN). Keep this number safe! You will need this number if you need to update or renew your registration at any time in the future.

In the Point of Contact field, once you have filled out the names of your company's Points of Contact, you will be asked to create a Marketing Partners Identification number, or MPIN. This number acts as your password and allows you access to many different government sites. This number is discussed in more detail later in this section. Keep this number safe!

In the Appendix section of this book you will find a copy of the worksheet provided by the Central Contractor's Registration, designed to help you gather all the information you will need before you submit your registration online. This includes information on your company type (corporate entity, sole proprietor, and so on) your business type (small, large, woman-owned business, and so on) financial information for Electronic Funds Transfer (Remember that the federal government will use the information you provide here to pay your invoices, so make sure the information is correct!) as well as the names of the people in your company who will be the Point of Contact concerning these matters. If any of this information changes, make sure you update your registration.

MARKETING PARTNERS IDENTIFICATION NUMBER (MPIN)

The Marketing Partner Identification Number (MPIN) allows you access to many government applications, and acts as your password in these cases. In addition, the MPIN number is now mandatory for all CCR registrations.

If you are already registered in CCR you can click on "Update or Renew Registration" and enter the system using your DUNS number and your TPIN number.

Go to the "Point of Contact" section and fill out these fields. At the end of this section you will be able to create your own MPIN number.

The MPIN that you create must have nine digits, with at least one number and at least one alpha character, with no special characters or spaces.

Click "Validate/Save."

Your MPIN number will be valid in 24 hours.

COMMERCIAL AND GOVERNMENT ENTITY (CAGE) CODES

The Commercial and Government Entity (CAGE) Code is a five-character identifier that is used extensively within the federal government. This code is unique to your company. It *must* appear on every contract and invoice. It is five digits long, made up of letters and numbers (for example: A123B). This code is used to identify your company for payment purposes.

You must have a separate CAGE Code for each physical location and separate division at the same physical location. Each separate CCR registration must have its own CAGE Code

If you are a U.S. company and you do not have a CAGE Code, then one will be assigned to you when you register at CCR.

If you think you already have a CAGE Code, search the Defense Logistics Information Service (DLIS) Website at *www.dlis.dla.mil/cage_welcome.asp.*

If you would like to find out another company's CAGE code, go to this site: *www.bpn.gov/bincs/begin_search.asp.*

NORTH AMERICAN INDUSTRIAL CLASSIFICATION SYSTEM (NAICS)

The government uses the North American Industrial Classification System (NAICS) numbers to identify the standards for a Small Business Set-Aside. You will find this number in the latest edition of the NAICS book or on the government Website. You must supply at least one NAICS number in order to complete your CCR registration.

The NAICS Manual is available for purchase, or you may search the manual at their Website. Simply click on the section "More Ways to Find Any NAICS Code—Electronic Manual" that you can see in the above page.

Website address: *www.naics.com*

STANDARD INDUSTRIAL CLASSIFICATION (SIC) CODES

When you register at the Central Contractors Registration site you will be asked to list all the Standard Industrial Classification (SIC) codes that apply to your products and services. Be sure to list as many as apply. SIC codes can be four or eight digits, all numeric. You must supply at least one valid SIC code for your registration to be complete.

If you do not know your SIC codes, you may perform a search at the Occupational Health and Safety Administration's (OSHA) Website: *www.osha.gov/pls/imis/sicsearch.html.*

FEDERAL SUPPLY CLASSIFICATION CODES (FSC) CODES

The government purchases 20 percent of all the products and all the services produced in the United States. Each product and each service is assigned a specific Federal Supply Classification (FSC) code.

- Product codes are number codes, from 10 through 99.
- Service codes are letter codes, from A to Z.
- Each code is further sub-divided, in order to give an exact description of the item.

At the FedBizOpps Website (*www.fbo.gov*), click on the "Advanced Search" option and scroll down to "Search by Procurement Classification,"Below this section you will see a link to "Additional Information on Classification Codes."

On the "Additional Information" page you will see a list of all the Product and Service Codes. Services are given a letter code, A through Z. Product categories are given a numerical code, from 10 to 99.

For example:

- 26—Tires and Tubes
- 39—Material Handling Equipment
- 65—Medical Equipment and Supplies
- D—Information Technology Services
- R—Professional Administrative Services
- T—Printing Services

The Defense Logistics Agency publishes a manual known as the "H2 Manual," which lists each of these codes in detail. The H2 Manual lists all these codes, and further sub-divides each one into more specific areas.

For example, Code S is used for Utilities & Housekeeping Services. This is further sub-divided, so that Code S201 is described as Custodial-Janitorial; Code S208 is for Landscaping Services; and Code S209 is reserved for Laundry and Dry Cleaning Services.

Product Codes are also similarly sub-divided. For example, Category 84 is used for Clothing items, and this is sub-divided so that 8430 is for men's footwear, 8450 is for children's clothing, and 8475 is for specialized flight clothing.

The H2 Manual is available at *www.dlis.dla.mil/pdfs/h2.pdf.*

 ONLINE REPRESENTATIONS AND CERTIFICATIONS (ORCA)

Until recently, each and every bid that you submitted to the federal government had to be accompanied by a document called Representations and Certifications. This document allowed you to self-certify the size of your company, if it was eligible for any set-aside programs, and so on.

In 2005, the government initiated the Online Representations and Certifications Application (ORCA) program, which allows you to certify your company profile electronically. You will be required to renew your registration annually. You may update your company's information at any time.

The Website address is *http://orca.bpn.gov*.

To log in to this program, you will need your Dun & Bradstreet (DUNS) number as well as the Marketing Partners Identification Number (MPIN) that you created when you registered at the Central Contractors Registration (CCR) site.

You will be asked to certify that you have read and understand certain regulations that apply to government contracting, such as fair-labor practices laws, non-discrimination laws, equal opportunity laws, and so on. The links to the left take you directly to the specific Federal Regulation that applies.

Provision	
52.203-2	Certificate of Independent Price Determination
52.203-11	Certification and Disclosure Regarding Payments to Influence Certain Federal Transactions
52.204-3	Taxpayer Identification
52.204-5	Women-Owned Business (Other Than Small Business)
52.209-5	Certification Regarding Debarment, Suspension, Proposed Debarment, and Other Responsibility Matters
52.212-3	Offeror Representations and Certifications - Commercial Items (Alternate 1 & 2)

You will further certify that you have not been de-barred or suspended, and that no money was used to influence government employees.

There are also provisions concerning veterans' employment and reporting requirements, and many others. You should take the time to read and understand each provision before you proceed.

In the next section, much of the information will have already been filled in for you. The ORCA program takes the information that you provided when you registered at the Central Contractor Registration (CCR) site and transfers that information here—for example, your Tax Identification Number (TIN), the type of organization, size of your company, and so forth. If you find that any of this information is incorrect, you will need to return to CCR and update your records there, before returning to the ORCA registration. Allow about 24 hours for the updates in CCR to show up on the ORCA site.

As with your CCR, you will be able to save a partially-completed record and return to it at a later date.

Once you have submitted your ORCA application, you will be able to save a copy for your own records.

A CHECKLIST FOR YOU

As you can see, there are many important codes that you will need to keep safe in order to do business with the federal government. Use this table to keep all your company's information together in one place.

Government Code	Description	My Records
SBA Size Standards	The Small Business Administration's size standards determine your company's eligibility as a small business.	
DUNS Number	The Dun & Bradstreet number certifies that your company is financially capable of fulfilling its obligations.	
TIN Number	Tax Identification Number.	
CCR Registration	Registration at the Central Contractors Registration Website is mandatory for all government contracting.	
TPIN Number	The Trading Partners Identification Number is assigned to you by CCR once your registration is complete.	
MPIN Number	The Marketing Partners Identification Number is created by you when you register at CCR. This number acts as your company password.	
CAGE Code	The Commercial & Government Entity code is unique to each division and each location of your company.	
NAICS Codes	The North American Industrial Classification Code identifies your company's general type of business.	
FSC Codes	Federal Supply Classification codes identify the specific items you can supply.	
SIC Codes	Standard Industrial Classification codes identify specific items you can supply.	
ORCA Registration	Online Representations and Certifications site. Renew the information at this site annually, or whenever company information changes.	

CHAPTER 2

SEARCHING THE FEDERAL BUSINESS OPPORTUNITIES (FEDBIZOPPS) WEBSITE

AN OVERVIEW

This chapter takes you step-by-step though the Federal Business Opportunities Website, otherwise known as FedBizOpps. The FedBizOpps Website is the single government point-of-entry for federal government procurement opportunities greater than $25,000. At this site you can search, monitor, and retrieve opportunities solicited by the federal contracting community

Searching. We take you step-by-step through the FedBizOpps procurement site. We show you how to search for business opportunities, and fully explain the results of the search so you can understand exactly what you see. Each term is explained in plain language, so that you understand exactly what the government is looking for—Synopsis, Solicitation, Pre-Solicitation, Modification, Amendment, Sources Sought, and more. We discuss how to narrow your search so that you find only those opportunities for which you are fully qualified. Once you have found an opportunity that interests you, we explain clearly the different documents that you must examine in detail in order to know the exact terms and conditions of this bid, and the red flags that could determine whether or not you place a bid—Technical Data Packages, Statements of Work, and so on.

Set-Aside Programs. In the next section we discuss the Set-Aside programs for small, very small, small disadvantaged 8(a), woman-owned, veteran-owned, minority-owned, and HUB-zone businesses. We clearly define each of these set-asides, and give you links where you can get more details of each of these programs.

Other Government Programs. We explain some other programs that you may come across when you search this site, and look at how they may affect your ability to place an offer—Sole Source, Qualified Products Lists, Federal Acquisition Regulations (FAR), shipping and packaging requirements, and so on.

THE FEDERAL BUSINESS OPPORTUNITIES WEBSITE

When any agency is going to make a purchase that is estimated to be $25,000 or more, then they are required to advertise that information at a Website called Federal Business Opportunities or FedBizOpps.

This information is found at the Website *www.fbo.gov.*

THE FEDERAL BUSINESS OPPORTUNITIES (FEDBIZOPPS) HOMEPAGE

Once you are at this Website, in the top left-hand corner there is a Quick Search option. Use this is option if you are looking for a specific solicitation and you know the solicitation number. Otherwise, click on Advanced Search.

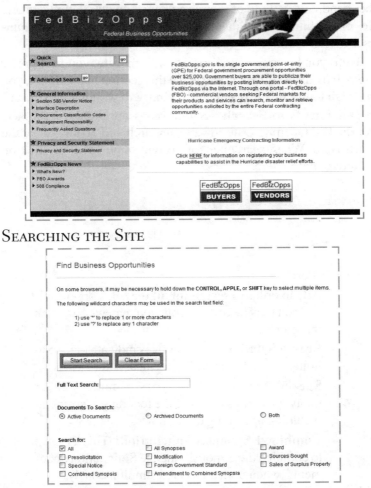

SEARCHING THE SITE

The Full Text search field supports keyword searches and Boolean search strings using *and*, *or*, and parentheses. You may enter the keywords either with or without parentheses. If you do not use quotation marks around your keyword, the site will search for root words in addition to the exact word you entered.

For example, if you sell metal, typing the word *Iron* will turn up clothes irons and ironing boards as well as metal products! On the other hand, this method of searching may help you to find suitable sales opportunities that you may miss completely if the opportunities are listed under FSC codes that you do not expect.

Until you become more familiar with the site, you may prefer to search by the FSC codes, and leave this section blank. Later, you may wish to use this text search capability to widen your search.

Documents to Search—Solicitations are archived 30 days after the Bid Opening Date. Awards are archived 30 days after the Award Date. When searching for current opportunities, click on the Active button here.

Search for:		
☑ All	☐ All Synopses	☐ Award
☐ Presolicitation	☐ Modification	☐ Sources Sought
☐ Special Notice	☐ Foreign Government Standard	☐ Sales of Surplus Property
☐ Combined Synopsis	☐ Amendment to Combined Synopsis	

Search For:

- **All:** In order to search for all the sales opportunities that may be open to you, you may wish to click this button.

- **Pre-Solicitation:** These notices indicate that a Solicitation will be issued in the near future.

- **Special Notices:** These types of notices cover many different aspects of the federal government, including upcoming trade shows.

- **Combined Synopsis/Solicitation:** This is used to combine the Synopsis and the Solicitation documents, when both are issued simultaneously.

- **Synopsis:** This is a brief description of the items that will be in the solicitation.

- **Modifications:** The term "Modification" is used to notify you of any changes to a previously issued

Synopsis document. The term "Amendment" is used when there are changes to a solicitation document that has already been issued. Both Amendments and Modifications can change specifications or due dates for offers, or could even cancel the request completely. If you decide to submit an offer, *always* check the Website for any Modifications or Amendments before you proceed, as they could significantly alter the details of the bid.

- **Foreign Government Standards:** These notices could be relevant if you are planning to ship an item overseas.

- **Amendment:** See "Modifications."

- **Award:** This option allows you to find out the details of a bid once it has been awarded.

- **Sources Sought:** The government is asking for potential suppliers of a particular product or service, but no specific solicitation is currently planned.

- **Sales of Surplus Property:** The government occasionally conducts sales of items that are surplus to their requirements.

METHODS OF SEARCHING

- **Search by Solicitation/Award Number:** If you know this number, you can insert this here. Otherwise leave this box blank

> Search by Solicitation / Award Number:

- **Dates to Search:** You can search for sales opportunities issued over the last three days, or you can go back as far as the last two months.

Dates to Search (mm/dd/yyyy):

From [   ]   To [   ]

| All Days |
| Last 3 Days |
| One Week |
| Two Week |
| Three Week |

- **Search by Place of Performance Zip Code:** If you wish to limit your searches to a specific geographical area, then you can do so in this box. Simply insert the relevant zip code. You may search by a complete 5-digit zip code, or by a grouped search. For example, either zip code 22000 or zip group 22*. For searches by a particular state, use the Full Text search field, using the product keyword and the state.

If you do not wish to limit your searches in this way, simply leave this box blank.

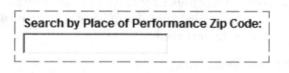

Search by Place of Performance Zip Code:

[   ]

- **Search by Set-Aside Code:** If you wish to limit your searches to any of the set-aside categoriesfor which you qualify, you can do so here. You can choose to search for all opportunities that are available to you, or limit your search; for example, to only the partial or total Women-Owned Small Business Set-Asides. The most common category here would be "Small Business Set-Aside," which represents approximately 20 percent of all sales opportunities available on a daily basis.

A more detailed description of the Set-Aside program is given later in this chapter.

Search by Set-Aside Code:

| All Codes |
| 8a Competitive |
| N/A |
| Partial HBCU |
| Partial HUB-Zone |

- **Search by Procurement Classification Code:**
  In the previous chapter we discussed the Federal
  Supply Codes (FSC) and how to find the specific
  category for your product or service. Highlight your
  category code here. If you have more than one
  code you will have to search for each one separately, unless the numbers are contiguous, in which
  case you will be able to use the Shift button to
  highlight more than one at a time.

Additional Information on Classification Codes: As we discussed in the previous chapter, this link gives you additional information on the Classification codes.

For more details, please go to Chapter 1, under the section
titled Important Business Codes and Numbers—The Federal Supply Classification (FSC) Codes.

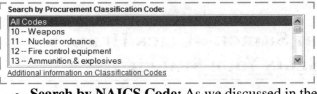

Search by Procurement Classification Code:

| All Codes |
| 10 -- Weapons |
| 11 -- Nuclear ordnance |
| 12 -- Fire control equipment |
| 13 -- Ammunition & explosives |

Additional information on Classification Codes

- **Search by NAICS Code:** As we discussed in the
  previous chapter, your company's products and
  services are all classified under the North American Industrial Classification System. If you wish
  to search using these numbers, then use this box.

Search by NAICS Code:

| All Codes |
| 111 - Crop Production |
| 112 - Animal Production |
| 113 - Forestry and Logging |
| 114 - Fishing, Hunting and Trapping |

Filter NAIC

- The Filter NAIC option further sub-divides the categories. For example, NAICS Code 238 is "Specialty Trade Contractors," which is sub-divided as shown above.

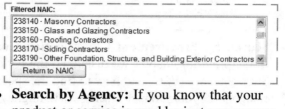

- **Search by Agency:** If you know that your product or service is used by just one agency, highlight only the agencies you wish to see. Otherwise click on All Agencies.

At the FedBizOpps Homepage, you can click on the Vendors button to obtain a listing of all agencies that post to this site. Each agency listing can also be further divided by office location if necessary.

START SEARCH — CLICK HERE TO BEGIN YOUR SEARCH.

 SEARCH TIPS

- When you are searching in FedBizOpps, if you open any of the search results in order to see the solicitation details, be aware that when you return to the Search page you will find that the system has automatically reset your search options, and if you wish to continue searching you will need to set the search parameters again.

- FedBizOpps is used as a central site where all federal buying agencies can notify you of a bid opportunity, but often the details of the bid are posted at the agency's own site.

In the "Additional Information" section of the synopsis, you may come across a link that takes you directly to the agency's site. If this link does not work try going directly to the agency site. For example, there are often links to the Defense Supply Centers in Richmond, Columbus, or Philadelphia, known as the DIBBS Website. This site is discussed in detail later in this book. If you still cannot access the site, send an e-mail to the Contracting Officer listed in the Synopsis, asking for the information.

- Always search FSC Code 99 "Miscellaneous" in addition to your other searches—you will be amazed at what you can find there!

- The quantity that you see listed in the Synopsis document may not be the entire amount that the agency wishes to purchase.

In this example you can see that in the FedBizOpps notice the quantity is listed as 21.

Proposed procurement for NSN 2520011368717 SHIFTERFORK,VEHICU: Line 0001 Qty 00021

However, once you find the solicitation document in DIBBS, you can see that the actual quantity requested is 120.

Click on the Solicitation # to view the RFQ & NSN/Part No. to view additional info.

	NSN/Part No. Nomenclature	Technical Documents Bid set/ Drawings	Spec/ Stnd	Solicitation #	Auction Status	PR # PR QTY	Issue	Return By
1	2520-01-136-8717 SHIFTERFORK, VEHICU	None	None	SPM7L2-07-T-2809 **Q** uote		0013612620 QTY: 120	1/5/2007	01/19/2007

Page: 1

If you click on the link to the solicitation and scroll through the document you will see that Line Item #1 is for a quantity of 21, and Line Item # 2 is for an additional quantity of 99.

LINE ITEM 0001			
PURCHASE REQUEST	QUANTITY	UNIT OF ISSUE	UNIT PRICE
0013612620	21	EA	

LINE ITEM 0002			
PURCHASE REQUEST	QUANTITY	UNIT OF ISSUE	UNIT PRICE
0013612620	99	EA	
PACKAGING DATA			

There are several reasons why this occurs.

One of the most common reasons is that First Article Testing is required to ensure the item is satisfactory before the remainder of the order is shipped. In that case Line Item #1 would be for an initial quantity for quality testing (often just a single unit) and Line Item #2 would be for shipment of the remaining quantity at a later date. (In certain cases you will see a notice that First Article Testing or FAT has been waived for certain manufacturers and part numbers.)

Another reason for this quantity discrepancy is when the items are going to be shipped to different locations. This is the case in this example, where 21 items are to be shipped to Pennsylvania and the remaining 99 items will be shipped to California.

```
                              SHIPPING DATA
        PARCEL POST/FREIGHT ADDRESS:
        W25G1U
        SU TRANSPORTATION OFFICER
        DDSP NEW CUMBERLAND FACILITY
        2001 MISSION DRIVE DOOR 113 134
        NEW CUMBERLAND PA 17070-5001
        US

                              SHIPPING DATA
        PARCEL POST ADDRESS:
        W62G2T
        XU DEF DIST DEPOT SAN JOAQUIN
        TRANSPORTATION OFFICER
        PO BOX 960001
        STOCKTON CA 95296-0130
```

On other occasions, different line items may be used when there are different delivery times. For example an agency may request a specific number of units delivered in 30 days, followed by additional units at a later date.

In the case of contracts that are for one year with several option years, the solicitation will list each year on a separate line. You will be able to supply pricing for the initial year and a separate pricing for any option years.

INTERPRETING THE SEARCH RESULTS

Once you click on the Search button, a list of announcements will appear. When you click on a notice that is of interest, you will find that they may contain various options. For example:

- Pre-Solicitation Notice.
- Synopsis.
- Solicitation document.
- Amendment and Modification.
- Technical Data Package (TDP).
- Award Notice.

In this example, you can see that there are several listings for you to read, including a Synopsis, an Amendment, a Modification, and an Award.

Search Results

Matching Documents Grouped by Organization and Posted Date

(Links may not be active for 1-2 hours after they first appear)

Active Postings: 6/115836   Page `1` of **1**

January 10, 2006

Agency:	Department of the Air Force
Office:	Air Force Materiel Command
Location:	96th Contracting Squadron (Eglin AFB)
➡**Posted:**	January 10, 2006
Type:	Synopsis
Title:	51 -- Aircraft Mechanic Tool Kits
SOL:	F1T0CW5332A1

Location:	Hill AFB OO-ALC
➡**Posted:**	January 10, 2006
Type:	Amendment 01
Title:	51--TOOL, KIT, BOMB SYSTEM
SOL:	FA8213-06-Q-60418

➡**Posted:**	January 09, 2006
Type:	Modification 01
Title:	51 -- Bearing Locknut Wrench Adapter
SOL:	6FLSB-N7-011786327

➡**Posted:**	January 09, 2006
Type:	Award
Title:	51 -- Hardware SuperStore
Award Number:	GS-06F-0017S

By clicking on Solicitation # FA8213-06-Q-60418, we can see that there have been three notices posted about this opportunity: the original Synopsis, followed by the actual Solicitation document, and finally the Technical Data Package, or TDP.

At this stage you would probably be interested in looking at the Synopsis, which should give you enough information about the requirements for you to decide that you will be able to supply the item.

Later, once you have decided that you are able to supply this item, you will need to click on the Technical Data Package.

Solicitation 01(*Posted on Dec 14, 2005*)

Description	Size (Bytes)	File Format
Solicitation	561,468	RTF (Rich Text Format)
Attachment - Spec & SOW	270,068	Adobe PDF
Attachment - EDR	23,599	Adobe PDF
Attachment - EDL	56,474	Adobe PDF
Attachment - CDRL	243,882	Adobe PDF
All Files	610,464	Zip Compression

Technical Data Package (TDP) 01(*Posted on Dec 15, 2005*)

Description	Size (Bytes)	File Format
Updated information available online via FedTeDS. This link leads to a page outside of the FedBizOpps system	N/A	N/A

Amendment 01(*Posted on Jan 10, 2006*)

Description	Size (Bytes)	File Format
Amendment 1	79,247	RTF (Rich Text Format)
All Files	8,296	Zip Compression

In the previous example, when I clicked on the link, this page appeared. You can see that there are many links to Attachment documents, Specification documents and Statements of Work (SOW), a Technical Data Package link, and an Amendment. You will need to read and understand each of these documents before you submit your offer. Any questions you may have can be answered by the Contracting Officer. Any Amendments or Modifications must be included in your submission.

Solicitation number : SP0560-03-R-0187
Title : 53 -- Digital Combination Locks - FSC 5340

Synopsis - Posted on Jul 24, 2003

Modification 01 - Posted on Jul 24, 2003

Solicitation 01 - Posted on Jul 31, 2003

Award - Posted on Aug 21, 2003

UNDERSTANDING THE SYNOPSIS

In this example, you can see that the Synopsis, a brief description of the item required, was posted on July 24th. Later that same day, a Modification was made. The following week the Solicitation document was issued. (This is the document you complete in order to make your offer, and we discuss this in detail later in the book .) An Award was made approximately 30 days after the Synopsis was issued. The time between the issuing of the Synopsis and the Award can vary.

When you find an opportunity that interests you, click on Synopsis to see more details of the requirement.

The following example is a typical Synopsis. It contains all the information you need in order to make a decision whether or not you are interested in submitting an offer.

53 -- Digital Combination Locks - FSC 5340

At the beginning of the Synopsis you have several key pieces of information.

You can see that the purchasing agency in this case is the Defense Logistics Agency.

The product description is Digital Combination Locks.

Federal Supply Classification Code 53 is identified as Hardware and Abrasives.

Federal Supply Classification 5340 is Commercial Hardware.

GENERAL INFORMATION

General Information	
Document Type:	Presolicitation Notice
Solicitation Number:	SP0560-03-R-0187
Posted Date:	Jul 24, 2003
Archive Date:	Aug 23, 2003
Original Response Date:	Aug 08, 2003
Current Response Date:	Aug 08, 2003
Classification Code:	53 -- Hardware & abrasives
SetAsides:	Total Small Business
Naics Code:	N/A

Document Type: A Pre-Solicitation notice is issued when the Solicitation is not yet available, but will be issued shortly. Other documents types are: Combined Synopsis/Solicitation, Request for Information, Sole Source, Request for Quote, Invitation for Bid, Request for Proposal, Modification, Amendment, Technical Data Package, and so on. These were discussed in Chapter 1.

Solicitation Number: This number will be used throughout the bidding process, unless an Amendment or Modification is issued to change it.

Posted Date: The date this notice was posted at this Website.

Original/Current Response Date: This is the date your bid must be submitted, once the solicitation becomes available. At times the original response date is extended and a new date is posted. Sometimes the notice of an extension of the due date will be given in an Amendment or Modification document. The actual response date will be in the solicitation when it is issued, and could be different from this date.

Original/Current Archive Date: This is the date that this synopsis will no longer appear at this site, unless you specifically search for it using the "Archive" search button.

Classification Code: Hardware and Abrasives.

Set-Aside: This bid has been set aside for small businesses only.

NAICS Code: In this particular case the North American Industrial Classification System (NAICS) code is not given, but in many cases it will be listed here.

CONTRACTING OFFICE ADDRESS

In this example we can see that the agency buying the Digital Combination Locks is the Defense Logistics Agency in Philadelphia. This office is part of the Defense Supply Center, which has operations in Philadelphia, Richmond, and Columbus.

Description:

Solicitation Number: SP0560-03-R-0122 FSC: 5340 Nomenclature: Digital Combination Locks RFP: Issue Date 31 JULY 2003 The solicitation is for a Firm Fixed Price Contract to be awarded under Commercial Procedures. This procurement is a total set-aside for small business. The procurement is for 2 competitive NSNs. The first NSN is 5340-01-498-2758, second NSN is 5340-01-498-2759. The total estimated value for the 2 items is $2,316,600.00. This procurement also contains an option to Increase Quantity Clause. Drawings are available at time of solicitation. Delivery is as follows: 60 day delivery to stock after date of order. The first NSNs is Qualified Products List (QPL) item, the second NSN has a FAT (First Article Test) requirement. Source Inspection requirements apply as contained in the solicitation. NOTE: Copy of this solicitation can be found on the DLA Procurement Gateway on the issue date 31 July, 2003 at http://progate.daps.dla.mil. Vendors must be a registered user and have valid user ID and password to access the procurement gateway. In order to download and view these documents, you will need the latest version of Adobe Acrobat Reader. This software is available free at http://www.adobe.com. For additional information, please contact Tarra Power, PAABA/13 @ 215-737-3530 or email a request to Tarra.Power@dla.mil.

This part of the Synopsis gives you a brief description of the product the agency is looking for. There were several key pieces of information in here:

Issue Date: The date the solicitation will be issued—in this case July 31st.

Firm Fixed Price Contract: This is a delivered price, valid throughout the term of the contract, which is not subject to change. At other times a contract may allow an Economic Price Adjustment, especially if it is a long-term, multi-year contract.

Commercial Procedures: Military and Federal regulations are not involved with this product.

National Stock Number: The 13-digit NSN fully identifies the product.

Full description of the item: This will be displayed in the bid package.

Estimated Value: The agency has given an estimated amount of the award, in dollars (in this case $2,316,600). This dollar amount is based on the previous award for this product.

Option to increase quantity clause: In the solicitation package you will find the percentage of estimated volume that the agency has the option to increase, with no price adjustment.

Drawings will be available in the bid package: Later, we will discuss in more detail how to obtain drawings and specifications.

Delivery dates: In this case delivery is required 60 days after the contract has been awarded. You may also see the terms ARO or ADO (After Receipt/ Delivery of Order) or ARC (After Receipt of Contract) used here.

Qualified Products List: This is discussed in more detail later in this chapter.

First Article Testing: You will initially ship only one item to the agency, which will ensure that it is satisfactory before the remainder of the order is shipped. Occasionally you will see that this requirement is waived for certain manufacturers and part numbers.

Source Inspection: The agency has the option to inspect the product at the place where it is being manufactured, prior to award.

Point of Contact: Here is the person to contact with any questions you may have about this bid.

Here is another example of a descriptive section of a solicitation, with more terms to understand:

> The solicitation will be Unrestricted and will result in a Firm Fixed Price with EPA Adjustments under provisions of FAR Part 12. Qualified Products List QPL applies IAW specification # MIL G-25013E NOT 1 dated 02/20/03 amend # E. This is a synopsis for a commercial item in accordance with the procedures of FAR 5.201 and FAR 5.203. These are not Critical Safety Items (CSI) per SAMMS interrogation on 12/14/06. QAP 164 applies. MSDS and OSHA Hazardous Warning Labels are requirements. The solicitation does not contain progress payments. All NSNs are procured as fully competitive in accordance with military/federal specifications/standards and/or voluntary industry standards. Refer to Section L, Clause 52.211-9G13 for obtaining such data. The final contract award decision may be based on a combination of price, past performance, and other evaluation factors as described in this

solicitation. Surge requirements apply to all NSNs. A surge plan detailing how the surge quantity requirements will be met must be submitted along with offer.

Unrestricted: That is, there are no set-aside programs associated with this solicitation.

Firm Fixed Price: Under a Firm Fixed Price Contract the price you quote is fixed, and cannot be adjusted at a later date.

EPA Adjustments: Economic Price Adjustments allow for price increases or decreases over the life of the contract.

FAR Part 12: This is referencing the Federal Acquisition Regulations, which we discuss in detail later in the book.

Qualified Products List: See the section about QPL later in this chapter.

IAW specification # MIL: In Accordance With (IAW) Military Specifications. You will need to download the specification in order to understand the requirements. See the section on how to obtain drawings and specifications on page 68.

Critical Safety Items: These are parts whose failure would cause loss of life, permanent disability or major injury, loss of a system, or significant equipment damage; for example, aircraft or missile parts.

QAP 164: Quality Assurance Provisions. A full list of these provisions can be found at the Defense Supply Center Richmond Website: *www. dscr.dla.mil/userweb/qap/qaps.htm.*

MSDS and OSHA Hazardous Warning Labels, Material Safety Data Sheets, and Occupational Safety, and Health Hazardous Warning labels are required in this case.

Progress Payments: This clause allows the agency to assist a small business before the delivery of the final product or service described in the contract. They are used on fixed price contracts when the deliverable will take more time and money to produce than the contractor is able to finance with its own money.

Specifications and Standards: We discuss how to obtain specifications for Military, Federal, and Voluntary Industry standards later in this chapter.

Evaluation Factors: Although price may be a significant factor in the evaluation of offers, it is not the *deciding* factor. In many cases the final award decision will be based upon a combination of price, delivery, past performance, socioeconomic programs, and other evaluation factors as described in the solicitation document. This is known as the Best Value purchasing. Federal Acquisition Regulations clearly specify that all offers must be evaluated in accordance with the criteria set out in the solicitation document. For many commercial items, this can simply be a combination of technical, price, and past performance.

A **Technical Evaluation** would normally include examination of such things as product literature, product samples, technical features, and warranty provisions. Technical factors make sure that you fully understand the requirements and that you are capable of supplying the item. Relevant experience and past performance, a suitable management plan, company resources and the overall quality of the product will also be taken into consideration

If a factor other than price determines the basis for the award decision, the solicitation will state the relationship of price to the non-price factors. Other considerations may be for example, Life Cycle Costs, Energy Conservation and Efficiency Costs, and overall Multi-Year costs.

A Price Evaluation Adjustment or Price Evaluation Preference may be used to allow small disadvantaged businesses to be awarded the contract, even though their offer is up to 10 percent higher than another firm's offer.

Cascade Method of Evaluation: In some cases the solicitation will be issued as a set-aside for a particular type of small business; for example, a business located in a HUB-Zone. However, if there is inadequate competition at this level the contracting officer may decide to use a "cascade method" to award the contract. For example, the first priority for the award might be for HUB-Zone companies, but if there is not adequate competition at this level then the next priority might be for a service-disabled veteran-owned company, and so on. Adequate competition is considered to be at least two qualified offers from companies in any set-aside category.

Surge and Sustainment: This is defined as the ability to supply an increase in quantity or a faster delivery time if the agency requires it. A "Surge" would be the ability to quickly increase the quantity available if required, and a "Sustainment" would be your ability to sustain that increase throughout the contract period.

If Surge and Sustainment is required, the details will be clearly stated in the contract. If a Validation plan is required, it should clearly define how you intend to meet this requirement: how you will work with your suppliers, how you will arrange for transport and delivery of the items, and so on.

APPROVED SOURCES

Proposed procurement for NSN 3110011892803 BEARING,ROLLER,CYLINDR: Line 0001 Qty 00080 UI EA Deliver To: SU TRANSPORTATION OFFICER within 201 days ADO Approved sources are 36069 4069671; 52661 4061140; 52661 4062708; 52661 4069671; 77445 4061140; 77445 4062708; 77445 4069671; 78118 4061140. The solicitation is an RFQ and will be available at the link provided in this notice. Hard copies of this solicitation are not available. Specifications, plans, or drawings

> are not available. All responsible sources may submit a quote which, if timely received, shall be considered. Quotes may be submitted electronically.

In some cases, the agency has a number of "approved sources" for the particular manufactured part they are looking to purchase. These are listed using the 5-digit manufacturer's CAGE code followed by the part number. Using the Business Identification Number Cross-Reference System (BINCS) at *www.bpn.gov/bincs* or the Central Contractor Registration (CCR) Website at *www.ccr.gov* you can look up the manufacturers that are listed here.

Drawings and specifications are not available, as they will be proprietary to the manufacturer.

This is a great way to find sales opportunities if you are a distributor for manufactured parts!

If your company offers an alternate product you will need to apply for Source Approval at the agency. Although it will not be eligible for the current solicitation, once it has been evaluated and approved it may be included in the next procurement notice.

The Defense Supply Center Richmond has a Source Approval Booklet for Critical Safety Items at *www.dscr.dla.mil/userweb/ sarguide.doc*, which explains this procedure.

For non-critical items, you would need to contact the agency directly and ask for the details on where to send your request.

Other Mandatory or Preferred Sources

The Jarvits Wagner O'Day (JWOD) Program (Recently renamed "Ability One")

This is a mandatory source program that requires federal personnel to purchase certain products and services from agencies that employ those who are legally blind or have severe disabilities—that is, from the National Institutes for the Blind (NIB) and the National Institute for the Severely Handicapped (NISH).

The JWOD program supplies janitorial products, office products such as pens, binders, and paper goods, disposable cutlery, and medical supplies such as catheters and masks, as well as janitorial services, warehouse services, recycling, food services, laundry, and grounds maintenance.

You may wish to apply to become a distributor of JWOD products.

For a complete list of products and services, go to the JWOD Website at *www.jwod.com.*

The Federal Prison Industries—UNICOR

Federal Prison Industries (FPI) was set up to provide paid employment to prison inmates, mainly through the manufacture of products for the federal government, under the trade name UNICOR. More than 19,300 inmates are employed in more than 100 FPI factories at 71 prisons.

UNICOR manufactures products such as office furniture, clothing, beds and linens, electronics equipment, and eyewear. It also offers services including data entry, bulk mailing, laundry services, and printing, recycling, and refurbishing vehicle components.

Agencies need not purchase from Federal Prison Industries (FPI) unless it determines that their products or services provide best value. If FPI does not provide the best value, then the buying agency may purchase from other sources according to government procurement regulations.

For a complete list of products and services, go to *www.unicor.gov.*

SOLICITATIONS WITH DRAWINGS OR SPECIFICATIONS

Proposed procurement for NSN 3110001655996 BEARING,ROLLER,SELF-AL: Line 0001 Qty 00043 UI EA Deliver To: XU DEF DIST DEPOT SAN JOAQUIN within 85 Line 0002 Qty 00319 UI EA Deliver To: SU TRANSPORTATION OFFICER within 85 days ADO Line 0002 Qty 00319 UI EA Deliver To: SU TRANS-PORTATION OFFICER within 85 days ADO The solicitation is an RFQ and will be available at the link provided in this notice. Hard copies of this solicitation are not available. Digitized drawings and Military Specifications and Standards may be retrieved, or ordered, electronically.

> All responsible sources may submit a quote which, if timely received, shall be considered. Quotes may be submitted electronically.

In this example, no manufacturers or part numbers are cited, and you may download the drawings and specifications electronically. For solicitations from the Defense Logistics Agency (beginning "SPM") you can click on the link provided (or go directly to the site) and download the drawings or specifications.

For more details on how to download drawings and specifications, see the chapter on searching at the Defense Logistics Agency's **Internet Bid Board System** (DIBBS) site.

Other agencies will give you information on where you can download the drawings. For example, the Army's TACOM agency will often give details of where to find the drawings in the body of the solicitation document. Sometimes the drawings are restricted, and at other times they must be sent to you on a CD rather than sent electronically. Contact the Contracting Officer if you cannot find the drawings and feel that they should be available.

The Automated Best Value System (ABVS)

This is a computerized system that collects information on how well a vendor has fulfilled the terms of any previous contracts, and converts that into a numeric score. The contracting officer will use this information as an additional evaluation factor when making Best Value Award decisions.

The system looks at your company's performance in fulfilling government contracts during the previous 24 months. The score is a combination of how well you fulfilled the contract both in terms of the quality of your product and timeliness of delivery.

The Delivery Score is affected by any shipments that were not shipped or received in their entirety by the contract delivery date.

The Quality Score is affected by any products that do not pass inspection, or any products that were not packaged appropriately. Any discrepancies will be reflected in your ABVS score.

Even if you replace or repair a defective item, your score will still be affected.

If your records reflect negative quality data, they are listed with one of these Discrepancy Codes:

Discrepancy Codes

A1—A5	Stored Material Deficiencies
C1—C6	Supplies Damaged or with Expired Shelf-Life
L1—L8	Wood Product Deficiencies
P0—P8	Packaging Deficiencies
Q1—Q7	Product Quality Deficiencies
T1—T6	Technical Data Deficiencies
W0–W9	Wrong Item/Incomplete Item Shipped
X1—XL	Damaged Material

If you have no performance history, your score will be neutral—that is, you will not be evaluated either favorably or unfavorably. For more information on the ABVS go to *www.dscr.dla. mil/proc/abvm/abvm.htm.*

ADDITIONAL INFORMATION

The Past Performance Information Retrieval System (PPIRS) is the site on which government agencies note how well you performed on any awarded contract, and share this information among other government agencies. You can have access to your own records, and may comment upon anything in the report, but you do *not* have access to the records of other contractors. *www.ppirs.gov/*

POINT OF CONTACT

This section gives you the name, phone number, fax number, and e-mail address of the individual who is responsible for the administrative portion of this award. Contracting Officers are your best friends! These people can answer every question you might have in reference to this solicitation.

NUMBERED NOTES

> **Government-wide Numbered Notes**
> DLA-Specific Numbered Notes

If a Numbered Note is referenced in the Synopsis document, you may click on this icon to see the exact reference. There are many examples of these notes. Some of the most common are:

Numbered Note 1:   The proposed contract is 100 percent set-aside for Small Businesses.

Numbered Note 9:   Details of where to obtain military documents or specifications.

Numbered Note 22: The government will only purchase this item from a single source.

Other notes, specific to the Defense Logistics Agency (DLA), would also appear here, if that link was active.

REGISTER TO RECEIVE NOTIFICATION

When this icon appears, you can give your e-mail address and you will automatically receive notice of any changes or modifications that are issued concerning this synopsis/solicitation. However, you should still check the Website regularly for any changes, Amendments, or Modifications to the document. Do *not* rely on the automatic notification process!

UNDERSTANDING AMENDMENTS AND MODIFICATIONS

Amendments and Modifications are issued at the earliest possible time after a synopsis is issued. As we explained earlier in this chapter, the term "Modification" is used to notify changes to a Synopsis, whereas the term "Amendment" is used when there are changes to Solicitation packages. Both Amendments or Modifications can change specifications or due dates for offers, or could even cancel the request completely. The change can be as minor as a change in the solicitation number, or as major as cancellation of the entire solicitation. Amendments and Modifications are also used to extend the bid opening date, or to change the date or time of day that your offer must be received. They may be changes, additions, or cancellations to the original synopsis document. It is your responsibility to monitor the Website for Amendments and Modifications. *Any Amendments and Modifications that are issued relating to a specific solicitation* must *be submitted along with your offer, or you may not be in compliance, and your offer could be rejected simply because you did not submit them.*

Correction to announcement:

The Classification Code is hereby changed   FROM: W, Lease or Rental of Equipment TO: S, Utilities and Housekeeping Services.

The NAICS Code is hereby changed FROM: 333319, Water softening Equipment Manufacturing TO: 221310, Water Supply and Irrigation Systems.   The SB size standard for this code is $6,000,000.00.

Reminder: This requirement is for LEASE and SERVICE of RO units, water softeners, and water deionization equipment   It shall be awarded as a Service contract under the Service Contract Act (SCA).

All other Description information remains unchanged.

This is the Description section of the first Modification to this particular notice. Notice the Classification codes and North American Industrial Classification System (NAICS) codes have been changed. The change in these codes has also affected the Small Business Administration's size standard for small businesses.

The second Modification is simply a notice of a delay in the posting of the Solicitation document. The third Modification also changes the issue date for the solicitation.

Correction to announcement:

The anticipated award will be a Firm-Fixed-Price contract with a period of performance to be for a six-month base year and four (4) one-year option periods.

The Solicitation response date is now posted.

All other descriptive information remains unchanged.

The fourth Modification is a notice that the terms of the contract has changed. The contract will be a Fixed Price contract for a six-month base, followed by four option years. The original Synopsis had stated that the contract would be for one year, followed by four option years

This is the first section of the Amendment document. One thing to notice in block 11 is whether or not the due date for the receipt of offers has been extended. In this case, it has not.

Further down the page, in Block 14, you will find the details of the Amendment. The Contracting Officer's contact information is also listed so that you can ask questions about this, if you need to.

Later in the Amendment document, the exact changes that have been made are noted. Some of these changes might be very important to you, so you should make every effort to read and understand them before you make your offer. For example, paragraph C states that all Amendments must be acknowledged. This means that you *must* incorporate these documents into your submission package in order to be considered eligible for an award.

Each Amendment and Modification document needs to be read and understood before you submit your offer.

THE SITE VISIT

In this particular instance, a Site Visit was held to allow potential contractors to fully understand the requirements. An announcement of an impending site visit will be made in the Synopsis or Pre-Solicitation documents. If you are unsure of whether a Site Visit has been scheduled, you should ask the Contracting Officer.

After the visit, the details will be posted so that anyone can view details of the visit and who attended. This document could give you valuable information about potential competitors!

QUESTIONS AND ANSWERS

Also included in the Bid Package are any questions that the Contracting Officer received regarding this solicitation and the answers that were given. These are posted so that any potential offeror may view them.

Solicitation 01 *(Posted on Dec 14, 2005)*

Description	Size (Bytes)	File Format
1-1 SF 1449 Solicitation FA4801-05-R-0007	1,012,224	Microsoft Word
1-2 Attachment 1 PWS (includes App. A - App. E)	167,424	Microsoft Word
1-3 Appendix F Map 1	4,977,664	Microsoft Word
1-4 Appendix F Map 2	4,482,048	Microsoft Word
1-5 Appendix F Map 3	2,098,688	Microsoft Word
1-6 Appendix F Map 4	1,263,104	Microsoft Word
1-7 Appendix F Map 5	3,083,776	Microsoft Word
1-8 Appendix F Map 6	3,264,000	Microsoft Word
1-9 Appendix F Map 7	2,131,968	Microsoft Word
2-1 Appendix F Map 8	932,352	Microsoft Word
2-2 Appendix F Map 9	647,168	Microsoft Word
2-3 Appendix F Map 10	2,277,376	Microsoft Word
2-4 Appendix F Map 11	1,012,736	Microsoft Word
2-5 Appendix F Map 12	625,664	Microsoft Word
2-6 Attachment 2 Wage Determination	74,752	Microsoft Word
2-7 Attachment 3 Past Performance Questionnaire	49,152	Microsoft Word
All Files	25,960,515	Zip Compression

THE SOLICITATION PACKAGE

This particular Solicitation is for a Service contract, and there are many documents that need to be read and understood.

- *SF 1449:* This is the first page of the Solicitation document, and it must be completed in order to be considered for an award. We discuss this document in great detail later in the book

- *Attachment 1:* Statements of Work (SOW) or Performance Work Statements (PWS) are issued for service contracts, and they contain detailed descriptions of the work requirement, as well as details of the delivery timetable, security requirements, estimated work quantities, and detailed costing schedules.

- *Appendices:* In this case these contain maps that are relevant to this particular solicitation.

- *Attachment 2:* Wage Determinations. This attachment contains details of pay scales for various occupations. Federal Acquisition Regulation Part 22 describes how existing labor laws apply to government contracts. federal agencies must encourage contractors to cooperate with federal and state labor requirements such as Safety, Health and Sanitation, Maximum hours and minimum wages, Equal employment opportunity, Child and convict labor, Age discrimination, Disabled and Vietnam veteran employment, and Employment of the handicapped. Wage determinations are available at the Dept. of Labor's Website: *www.wdol.gov.*

- *Attachment 3:* Past Performance Questionnaire. This requires you to give reference details of your past customers.

We will discuss Service contracts and their specific requirements later in this book

THE SET-ASIDE PROGRAMS

The official definition of a particular set-aside will be included in the quote that you are offering. You may be eligible for several of these set-asides.

SMALL BUSINESS CONCERN

Eligibility for Small Business status is determined from information provided by the Small Business Administration (SBA). The Small Business Administration uses the North American Industrial Classification System (NAICS) to determine the types of industries and their size standards. One of two criteria is used to define a Small Business: either the average number of full-time employees during the last three years, or the average gross sales during the last three years. The NAICS codes and Small Business eligibility can both be found at the Small Business Administration Website: *www.sba.gov or at www.sba.gov/size.*

VERY SMALL BUSINESS CONCERN

According to the Code of Federal Regulations Part 121.413, a Very Small Business Concern is a business that contains an average of no more than 15 full-time employees during the last three years, and average annual receipts do not exceed $1 million.

WOMAN-OWNED BUSINESS CONCERN

This is a business that is at least 51-percent owned and controlled by a woman, who works in that company on a full-time basis.

SMALL DISADVANTAGED 8(*a*) BUSINESSES

The Small Business Administration (SBA) has several programs for small disadvantaged businesses. The 8(a) Program is designed to help firms that are socially or economically disadvantaged. Small Disadvantaged Business Certification relates specifically to federal procurement.

In order to qualify for these program, your company must be a small business, and it must be at least 51-percent owned by a U.S. citizen who is either socially or economically disadvantaged. The company must also have been operational for at least two full years.

A Socially Disadvantaged Individual is defined as someone who has been subjected to racial or ethnic prejudice or cultural bias. This includes Black Americans, Hispanic Americans, Native Americans, Asian Pacific Americans, and Subcontinent Asian Americans.

An Economically Disadvantaged Individual is defined as someone whose abilities to compete in the free enterprise system has been impaired due to diminished capital and credit opportunities.

Program participation is divided into two stages; the Developmental stage lasts for four years, and the Transitional stage lasts for five years. Your certification as an 8(a) business will be reviewed annually.

For more detailed information on the 8(a) program, go to the Website:

www.sba.gov/8abd.

For more information on the Small Disadvantaged Program, go to the website:

www.sba.gov/sdb/indexsdbapply.html.

MINORITY-OWNED AND
SMALL MINORITY-OWNED BUSINESSES

A Minority-Owned Business is any business, large or small, that is at least 51-percent owned and operated by a minority. A Small Minority-Owned Business is a small business that is at least 51-percent owned and operated by a minority.

HUB-ZONE BUSINESS

The HUB-Zone Empowerment Contracting program encourages economic development in Historically Underutilized Business Zones, or HUB-Zones. In order to qualify, a small business must be located in a HUB-Zone; it must be owned and controlled by a U.S. citizen; and at least 35 percent of its employees must reside in the HUB-Zone.

For more information about HUB-Zones, and to find out which areas are designated HUB Zones, go to *https://eweb1.sba.gov/hubzone/internet.*

VETERAN-OWNED AND SERVICE-DISABLED
VETERAN-OWNED BUSINESSES

A Veteran-Owned Business is a business of any size that is owned and operated by a certified veteran of the armed forces. A Service-Disabled Veteran-Owned Business is one that is owned and operated by a certified disabled veteran of the armed forces.

A Veteran is defined by the government as someone who has served in the active military, naval, or air service and who was discharged other than dishonorably.

A Service-Connected Disability means that the disability was incurred in the line of duty in the active military, naval, or air service.

A Service Disabled Veteran is a person who served in the active military, naval, or air service, whose disability was incurred or aggravated in line of duty in that service.

In order to be considered a Service Disabled Veteran, you must have an adjudication letter from the Veterans Administration; a Department of Defense Form 214, Certificate of Release or Discharge from Active Duty; or a statement of Service from the National Archivess and Records Administration stating that you have a service-connected disability.

You may request military personnel records from the offices in this link: *http://www.sba.gov/GC/FAQs-mar2005.pdf.*

A Service-Disabled Veteran-Owned Small Business Concern is a small business that must be at least 51-percent directly and unconditionally owned by one or more Service-Disabled Veterans. The management and daily business operations of the business must be controlled by one or more Service-Disabled Veterans. In addition, the Service-Disabled Veteran must hold the highest officer position in the business.

OTHER IMPORTANT PROGRAMS

SOLE SOURCE

A Sole Source solicitation is used when the government agency is only aware of a single company that is qualified to supply that product or service. However, if you believe that you can also supply this item, you may respond to the agency and submit a proposal. In the Sole Source notice, the agency will have to justify why they intend to purchase from only one source. The various reasons for purchasing from only one source may include:

- **Unusual and Compelling Urgency** (Federal Acquisition Regulation (FAR) 6.302-2): If the agency's need for a particular item or service is urgent, and delay in awarding the contract could result in serious injury, they are permitted to limit the number of sources for soliciting bids. The Contracting Officer will try to get verbal proposals from as many sources possible, but a formal solicitation document will not be issued. After the award has been made, the agency will publicize the requirement, so that they can identify any other sources for future bidding.

- **Specialized Knowledge or Expertise** (FAR 6.302-3): In some cases a particular contractor may have extensive knowledge of a particular area, or may have participated in drawing up standards or writing documentation for the agency. In this case, if the contract was awarded to another company, there would be unacceptable duplication of training costs and other possible delays.

- **International Agreement or Treaty** (FAR 6.302-4): Sole Source may be justified if full and open competition is precluded by the terms of an International Agreement or Treaty. In some cases a purchase will be reimbursed by a foreign country, and they may require that those products be obtained from a particular firm. For example, if the agency will be conducting business in another country, you may see solicitation notices where the contract will only be awarded to a firm from that country.

- **Authorized or Required by Statute** (FAR 6.302-5): Certain laws may require that the agency purchase a product or service from a particular source; for example from the Federal Prison Industries (UNICOR); the Association for the Blind or Severely Disabled (JWOD); or from companies participating in the Small Business Administration's Small Disadvantaged Business Program 8(a).

- **National Security** (FAR 6.302-6): Sole Source may be justified if the disclosure of the agency's needs would compromise the national security. However, this justification cannot be used merely because the acquisition is classified, or because access to classified matter will be necessary to submit a proposal or to perform the contract.

- **Public Interest** (FAR 6.302-7): Sole Source may be justified if the agency determines that full and open competition of a particular purchase is not in the public interest.

Justifications must be made in writing. The Contracting Officer must certify the accuracy of the justifications and obtain the necessary approvals before proceeding.

Qualified Products List (QPL)

In this case, the agency wants to buy a product from a supplier where the product has been commercially tested and certified by an independent laboratory to perform a specific task. If you are interested in determining whether your company is capable of producing a Qualified Products List item, then your first step would be to contact the Contracting Officer, whose contact information appears at the end of the Synopsis.

The Defense Supply Center Columbus (DSCC) has a master index of all their Qualified Products Lists (QPL) and Qualified Manufacturers Lists (QML), and they are available for download from the DSCC. These items are primarily from Federal Supply Codes 16, 25, 29, 30, 43, 47, 48, 59, 60, 61, 66, and 99.

www.dscc.dla.mil/programs/qmlqpl/

Qualified Suppliers List for Manufacturers (QSLM) and Distributors (QSLD)

The Defense Supply Center runs a program where manufacturers and distributors may pre-qualify to supply certain items to the agency. In order to pre-qualify you must show that your standard controls comply with certain criteria, which ensures that the products conform to specification requirements.

More information for some of the most common Qualified Supplier Lists include:

- Bulk Metals: QSL for Distributors.
- Class 3 Threaded Fasteners: QSL for Manufacturers and QSL for Distributors.
- Fiber Rope, Cordage, Twine, and Tape: QSL for Manufacturers and QSL for Distributors.
- Rivets: QSL for Manufacturers and QSL for Distributors.
- O-Rings: QSL for Manufacturers and QSL for Distributors.
- Class 2 Threaded Fasteners: Combined QSLM/QSLD.
- Quick Release Pins Combined QSLM/QSLD Criteria and Provisions.

For information on the companies who are currently on these lists, see the following Website: *http://phl1s157.dscp.dla.mil/qsl/qslmain.htm*

Specifications, Standards, and QPL lists can be found in the Department of Defense ASSIST database. You will need to create a user ID and password to access this information.

http://assist.daps.dla.mil/online/start/

OTHER GOVERNMENT AGENCY STANDARDS

Department of Energy (DOE)
www.hss.energy.gov/nuclearsafety/techstds/
Federal Aviation Administration (FAA)
http://ato-p.se-apps.faa.gov/faastandards/
National Aeronautics and Space Administration (NASA)
http://ato-p.se-apps.faa.gov/faastandards/

FEDERAL ACQUISITION REGULATIONS (FAR)

This is the *Bible* when it comes to federal government contracting! These regulations govern all federal agencies when they purchase supplies or services.

All solicitations follow the guidelines of various Federal Acquisition Regulations. These regulations are often referenced in the solicitation, but are not explained further. For a complete understanding of a particular regulation, you may request the information from the Contracting Officer, who will explain the regulation, send you a written copy of the regulation, or direct you to a Website. Any questions arising from the regulation can also be directed to the Contracting Officer. In many cases certain regulations that may have the most affect on the purchase of a product or service will be emphasized in the Synopsis document.

Federal Regulations are available on the Website: *http://farsite.hill.af.mil*.

In addition, each agency can issue their own supplements. For example:

The Department of Defense Supplemental Regulations (DFARS)

The Army's Supplemental Regulations (AFARS)

The General Services Administration Acquisition Manual (GSAM)

The following is a list of each part of the FAR, with a description of the scope of each section.

Part 1: Covers basic policies and general information about the Federal Acquisition Regulation System.

Part 2: Gives definitions of frequently used words and terms found in the FAR.

Part 3: Discusses how to avoid improper business practices and personal conflicts of interest

Part 4: Covers administrative matters related to a contract.

Part 5: Describes how the government publicizes contract opportunities and award information.

Part 6: Explains to federal buyers how to promote full and open competition in the acquisition process.

Part 7: Explains to federal buyers how to develop an acquisition plan; how to determine whether to use commercial or government resources; how to decide whether it is more economical to lease equipment rather than purchase it; and how to determine if a particular function is inherently governmental.

Part 8: Discusses the acquisition of supplies and services from government supply sources; for example from the Federal Prison Industries (UNICOR); the Committee for Purchase from People Who Are Blind or Severely Disabled (JWOD); and both the Mandatory and Optional Federal Supply Schedules.

Part 9: Looks at how the buyer may determine whether a contractor is fully qualified to provide the product or service. This section includes the contractor's responsibilities; debarment, suspension, and ineligibility; Qualified Products (QPL); First Article Testing (FAT); and Contractor Team Arrangements.

Part 10: Explains to the federal buyer how to conduct market research in order to find the most suitable approach for purchasing supplies or services.

Part 11: Covers the policies and procedures that are used when the agency describes exactly what it needs.

Part 12: Explains the policies and procedures that are unique to the acquisition of commercial items. The Federal Acquisition Streamlining Act of 1994 establishes acquisition policies that more closely resemble those found in the commercial marketplace, and encourages the acquisition of commercial items and components whenever possible.

Part 13: Describes how Simplified Acquisition Procedures are used when an agency is purchasing supplies and services that do not exceed the Simplified Acquisition Threshold of $100,000. (In certain instances the agency may obtain special authority to use these simplified procedures to acquire items that exceed this threshold.)

Part 14: Covers the requirements of contracting for supplies and services by sealed bidding; what information must be included in the solicitation; the procedures for the submission of bids; the requirements for opening and evaluating bids and awarding contracts; and the procedures for two-step sealed bidding.

Part 15: Covers the policies and procedures that govern negotiated acquisitions.

Part 16: Explains to the federal buyer the specific procedures that they must use when they select a contract type.

Part 17: Covers the acquisition of supplies and services through special contracting methods, including multi-year contracts, options, and so on.

Part 18: Identifies certain flexibilities that may be used to streamline the standard process in the event of an emergency acquisition.

Part 19: Discusses the Small Business Act. It covers eligibility, the roles of executive agencies and the Small Business Administration, as well as the various set-aside programs: subcontracting assistance programs, the "8(a)" program; women-owned small businesses; Price Evaluation Adjustments for Small Disadvantaged Businesses; Price Evaluation Preferences for HUB-Zone small businesses; the Small Disadvantaged Business Program; veteran-owned small businesses and Sole Source awards to HUB-Zone small businesses and service-disabled veteran-owned small businesses.

Part 20—Reserved

Part 21—Reserved

Part 22: Covers various labor laws and how they affect government acquisitions.

Part 23: Discusses environmental issues such as pollution control, efficient energy and water use, renewable energy, the purchase of energy- and water-efficient products and services, environmentally preferable products, products that use recovered materials and requirements for identifying hazardous materials.

Part 24: Discusses the Privacy Act of 1974 and the Freedom of Information Act.

Part 25: Discusses the acquisition of foreign supplies, services, and construction materials. It also covers the Buy American Act, trade agreements, and other laws and regulations.

Part 26: Looks at socioeconomic programs such as the Indian Incentive Program; Disaster or Emergency Assistance Activities; Historically Black Colleges/Universities and Minority Institutions.

Part 27: Discusses the regulations that pertain to patents, data rights, and copyrights.

Part 28: Discusses financial protection against losses; bid guarantees, bonds, alternative payment protections, security for bonds, and insurance.

Part 29: Explains the use of tax clauses in contracts, immunity or exemption from taxes, and tax refunds. This section is an explanation of how certain federal, state, and local taxes apply to federal government contracting. This is only for general information, and does not present the full scope of the tax laws and regulations.

Part 30: Discusses the Cost Accounting Standards Board rules and regulations in relation to negotiated contracts and subcontracts. This part does not apply to sealed bid contracts or to any contract with a small business concern.

Part 31: Explains cost principles and procedures for pricing contracts, subcontracts, and Modifications whenever cost analysis is performed.

Part 32: Looks at contract financing and payment methods, including partial payments and progress payments, loan guarantees, advance payments, contract funding, and so on. This section also discusses Electronic Funds Transfer or EFT.

Part 33: Discusses the procedures for filing protests and for processing contract disputes and appeals.

Part 34: Looks at the procedures that are used when an agency acquires major systems, and discusses the Earned Value Management System.

Part 35: Discusses procedures that apply to research and development (R&D) contracting.

Part 36: Discusses procedures that apply to construction and architect-engineer services.

Part 37: Looks at the procedures that are specific to service contracts. This part also discusses the use of performance-based acquisitions for services.

Part 38: Discusses the procedures for contracting for supplies and services under the Federal Supply Schedule programs that are managed by the General Services Administration (GSA); the Department of Veterans Affairs (for medical supplies) and the Department of Defense's schedule for military items.

Part 39: Looks at the procedures that apply in Information Technology and financial management system contracts.

Part 40—Reserved

Part 41: Looks at the procedures for the acquisition of utility services.

Part 42: Looks at the procedures that apply in contract administration and audit services.

Part 43: Discusses contract modifications for all types of contracts.

Part 44: Looks at the procedures for subcontracts.

Part 45: Discusses the procedures for providing government property to contractors.

Part 46: Looks at Quality Assurance issues, and how to ensure that supplies and services conform to quality requirements. Included are inspection, acceptance, warranty, and other measures associated with quality requirements.

Part 47: Looks at transportation and traffic management considerations in the acquisition of supplies. Also discusses acquiring transportation or transportation-related services.

Part 48: Looks at using and administering value engineering techniques in contracts.

Part 49: Discusses the termination of contracts, including termination of contracts for the convenience of the government or for default. This section also covers contract clauses relating to termination and excusable delay, as well as instructions for using termination and settlement forms.

Part 50: Discusses Extraordinary Contractual Actions, in which contracts are created, modified, or amended in order to facilitate the national defense.

Part 51: Looks at the use by contractors of Government supply sources, interagency fleet management system vehicles, and related services.

Part 52: Discusses how the buyer may use provisions and clauses in contracts, and how various FAR provisions and clauses are applicable to each contract type.

SOME COMMONLY LISTED FAR REGULATIONS

FAR 52.212-1, Instructions to Offerors—Commercial Items (Sep 2006)

FAR 52.212-2, Evaluation—Commercial Items (Jan 1999)

FAR 52.212-3, Offeror Representations and Certifications—Commercial Items (Sep 2006)—A Completed Copy of This Provision Shall be Submitted with Quotes

FAR 52.212-4, Contract Terms and Conditions—Commercial Items (Sep 2005)

FAR 52.212-5, Contract Terms and Conditions Required to Implement Statutes or Executive Orders—Commercial Items (Sep 2006)

FAR 52.29-6, Notice of Total Small Business Set-Aside (Jun 2003)

FAR 52.222-3, Convict Labor (Jun 2003)

FAR 52.222-19, Child Labor—Cooperation with Authorities and Remedies (Jan 2006)

FAR 52.222-21, Prohibition of Segregated Facilities (Feb 1999)

FAR 52.222-26, Equal Opportunity (Apr 2002)

FAR 52. 222-35, Equal Opportunity for Special Disabled Veterans, Veterans of the Vietnam Era, and Other Eligible Veterans (Sep 2006)

FAR 52.222-36, Affirmative Action for Workers with Disabilities (Jun 19998)

FAR 52.222-37, Employment Reports on Special Disabled Veterans, Veterans of the Vietnam Era, and Other Eligible Veterans (Sep 2006)

FAR 52.225-13, Restrictions on Certain Foreign Purchases (Feb 2006)

FAR 52.232-36, Payment by Third Party (May 1999)—An Award Can Only Be Made to Contractors Registered in Central Contractor Registration (*www.ccr.gov*)

DFARS 252.204-7004 Alt A, Central Contractor Registration (Nov 2003)

DFARS 252.212-7001, Contract Terms and Conditions Required to Implement Statutes or Executive Orders Applicable to Defense Acquisitions of Commercial Items (Oct 2006)

DFARS 252.225-7036, Buy American Act—Free Trade Agreements—Balance of Payments Program (Oct 2006), Alt 1.

THE CONTRACTING OFFICER

The final portion of the Synopsis contains the Government's point of contact, including a name, address, phone and fax number, and email address. This individual is your best friend! You can ask them anything about this Solicitation. It is their function to assist you in any area of this solicitation. They will have the answers to your questions, or they will tell you where to go to acquire the information.

RELATED LINKS

At the FedBizOpps homepage, there are links to other sites that can help you understand the marketplace.

BUSINESS PARTNER NETWORK

This site gives you access to several key data bases across Federal Agencies. *www.bpn.gov*

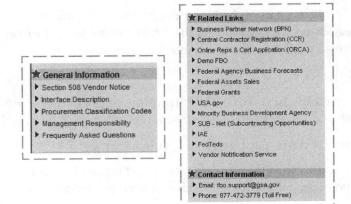

Federal Agency Business Forecasts

This section allows you access to individual agency sites, where you may search for forecasts of future procurements. *http://acquisition.gov/comp/procurement_forecasts/index.html*

Federal Assets Sales

At this site you can buy new, seized, and surplus government merchandise, either through online or public auctions or at a fixed price, through a sealed bid, or by contact. *www.usa.gov/shopping/shopping.shtml*

Federal Grants

This site has information on more than 1,000 grant programs, with access to approximately $400 billion in annual awards. By registering once on this site, your organization can apply for grants from 26 different federal agencies. *www.grants.gov*

USAGov

This is the U.S. government's official site, which is a wonderful source of information about federal government contracting, online information and resources. *www.usa.gov*

Minority Business Development Agency

This is a part of the U.S. Department of Commerce, and was created specifically to foster the establishment and growth of minority-owned businesses in America. *www.mbda.gov*

Sub-Net

Search here for subcontracting opportunities. *http://web.sba.gov/subnet/search/index.cfm*

Integrated Acquisition Environment (IAE)

At this site you can learn more about regulations, systems, resources, opportunities, and training. *www.acquisition.gov*

FedTeds

You will usually find yourself directed to this site if you need access to documents that are considered more sensitive. *www.fedteds.gov*

Vendor Notification Service

If you wish, you may sign up at this location to receive procurement announcements via e-mail. You may request notification of all notices posted for a particular solicitation number (amendments, modifications), or you may choose to receive notices from a particular organization, by Federal Supply Code (FSC), and so on. However, the service does not guarantee that you will receive these notifications, and you are still responsible for reviewing FedBizOpps for notices.

Section 508

This regulation requires that government agencies purchase electronic and Information Technology goods and services that are accessible by persons with disabilities.

A Product Accessibility Template allows you to describe how your particular product or service complies with this regulation. The template is available at: *www.access-star.org/ITI-VPAT-v1.2.html.*

More information on Section 508 is available at their Website: *www.section508.gov.*

Hurricane and Disaster Response Contracting

Also on the FedBizOpps homepage you will find information on contracting for natural emergency and disaster response purchases. Because of the urgent nature of these requirements the opportunities are unlikely to be posted to FedBizOpps or other official Websites.

During times of Natural Disasters, many products and services are needed for relief, cleanup, and restoration. If you supply products or services that may be needed to support the Hurricane Katrina effort, and you wish to be considered as potential sources of supply, you should send an e-mail to Katrinasupport@gsa.gov.

The Contracting Officers who are working with the Federal Emergency Management Agency (FEMA) during the hurricane relief effort are using the General Service Administration's e-library, GSA Advantage! and GSA e-Buy to find the products and services they need to support Hurricane Katrina relief and restoration efforts.

FedBizOpps Homepage — Vendor Link

Finally, in the FedBizOpps homepage, you will see a link for Vendors. If you click here you will be able to search for a particular agency by its acronym.

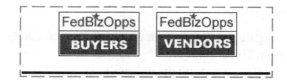

A Word on Acronyms

There are many acronyms used throughout the federal contracting arena. For further clarification you may wish to use these Websites. If in doubt, ask the Contracting Officer!

Defense Acquisition University: Defense Acquisition Acronyms and Terms

www.dau.mil/pubs/glossary/preface.asp

Defense Supply Center Columbus Acronyms

www.dscc.dla.mil/search/acronym/default.asp

CHAPTER 3

SEARCHING AND QUOTING IN THE DEFENSE LOGISTICS AGENCY'S INTERNET BID BOARD SYSTEM (DIBBS) WEBSITE

AN OVERVIEW

In this chapter we will take a close look at the Defense Logistics Agency's Internet Bid Board System, also known as DIBBS. At this site you will be able to search for sales opportunities and submit your quotes electronically. This site contains many smaller sales opportunities, and is a great way for you to "get your feet wet" with federal contracting. Although many of these sales opportunities are for small amounts, together they can add up to a BIG opportunity for your company!

Many of these sales opportunities are listed and awarded electronically, so that once you have completed a few of these bids, you will find that much of the work is repeated from bid to bid.

This chapter takes you step-by-step through searching the site, finding the sales opportunities, and submitting your quote online. We discuss the Procurement Automated Contract Evaluation (PACE) program; Approved part numbers; the Master Solicitation document; and the Automated Best Value System (ABVS).

93

This chapter also discusses the new cFolders system, which allows you access to technical data such as drawings and specifications, as well as the Quality Shelf Life program and the Defense Logistics Agency's commitment to environmental or "green" purchasing, via various programs.

Remember that not every sales opportunity requires you to know about all of these programs, but you may come across some of them as you begin to search this site.

In this chapter we also show you where you can find information on the purchasing history of an item—giving you valuable information about the company that supplied the item in the past and their unit delivered price, BEFORE you submit your offer!

Next we take you step-by-step through the online quoting system so that you can feel confident in submitting your offer electronically.

Finally, we show you how to track a solicitation, starting from when you first submit your offer until the final award is posted.

THE DIBBS HOMEPAGE

www.dibbs.bsm.dla.mil/

At the Defense Logistics Agency's Internet Bid Board System (DIBBS) you can search for sales opportunities, and submit quotes electronically.

Help
- **Help**
  - Frequently Asked Questions ~ FAQ
  - DIBBS On-Line Quoting Help
  - Batch Quoting Help
- Contact Us

Vendor Registration
- **Vendor Registration**
- Registration Guidelines

Solicitations
- Requests for Quotation (RFQ)
  - Batch Quoting
  - Submitted Quote Searching
- Requests for Proposal (RFP) / Invitation For Bid (IFB)
- Other DLA Opportunities

Awards
- Awards
- Other DLA Awards
- Subsistence Blanket Purchase Agreements (BPAs)

References
- Global Search
- Federal Stock Classes (FSC) managed by DLA
- Master Solicitation Documents
- Regulation Extracts used for DIBBS quoting
- Virtual Library
- Automated Best Value System (ABVS)
- Supplier Requirements Visibility Application

Technical Data
- DLA Collaboration Folders (cFolders)
- DLA Packaging
- DoD Specifications and Standards
- Military Engineering Data Asset Locator System

THE VENDOR TAB

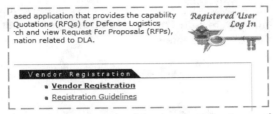

ased application that provides the capability
Quotations (RFQs) for Defense Logistics
·ch and view Request For Proposals (RFPs),
nation related to DLA.

Registered User Log In

Vendor Registration
- **Vendor Registration**
- Registration Guidelines

You will need to register at this site in order to receive a login account and password that will allow you to submit quotes. From the homepage, click the Vendor Registration link to begin the registration process. At the registration page you will also have the option to receive notification of solicitations for specific Federal Supply Codes (FSCs), National Stock Numbers (NSNs), or Approved Manufacturers that you select in your profile.

THE SOLICITATIONS TAB

Solicitations
- Requests for Quotation (RFQ)
    RFQ Auctions
    Batch Quoting
    Submitted Quote Searching
- Requests for Proposal (RFP) / Invitation For Bid (IFB)
- Other DLA Opportunities

Click on the Requests for Quotation (RFQ) link to begin searching for opportunities.

RFQs are simplified acquisitions under $100,000 and are available for online secure quoting.

■**Custom Queries**
  Search the RFQ Database.

■**Text Search**
  Search RFQ text for any word(s) or phrase(s).

RFQ Database Search

Search Categories:
National Stock Number (4)

Search Value(s): *

Reset   Submit »»

RFQ Text Search
Enter your query:

Modified: at any time.
Clear   Execute

Additional Text Search Help

You may search for opportunities using the Database Search, which allows you to search by National Stock Number (NSN) Federal Supply Code (FSC), solicitation number, Purchase Request number,

Nomenclature, manufacturer, or part number. Alternatively, you may use the Text Search option.

The Database Search option also allows you to narrow your search by the following categories.

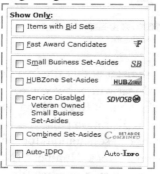

Fast Award bids have an estimated value of $2,500 or less, and they may be awarded *before* the return date on any automated solicitation. Because of this, you should submit your quote as soon as possible, rather than waiting until the due date.

You may also limit your search to only those solicitation documents that are set-aside for small businesses, businesses located in a HUB-Zone, Service-Disabled, veteran-owned small businesses, or a combination of all set-asides.

Auto-IDPOs are Indefinite Delivery, Indefinite Quantity (IDIQ) Purchase Orders that are estimated to be valued at less than the simplified acquisition threshold ($100,000). Auto-IDPO uses pricing logic and other automated filters to make fully automated IDPO awards. These awards do not specify an exact quantity of supplies other than a minimum quantity. Auto-IDPOs are awarded with a Base Year and one option year.

RFP/IFB DATABASE

From the homepage, you may also search for Requests for Proposals (RFP) and Invitations for Bids (IFB). These are large purchases, with an estimated value of $100,000 or greater. Click on this option to search for these opportunities.

OTHER DLA OPPORTUNITIES

Click here to see links to other Defense Logistics Agency sites where you may search, including Procurement Gateway, which is discussed in Chapter 4, as well as links to other specific Defense Supply Center sites:

DSCC—Defense Supply Center, Columbus.

DSCP—Defense Supply Center, Philadelphia.

DSCR—Defense Supply Center, Richmond.

UNDERSTANDING THE
SOLICITATION NUMBERING SYSTEM

The first four digits of a Defense Logistics Agency solicitation number is a site identifier:

SPM1   Defense Supply Center, Philadelphia—Clothing & Textiles.

SPM2   Defense Supply Center, Philadelphia—Medical.

SPM3   Defense Supply Center, Philadelphia—Subsistence.

SPM4   Defense Supply Center, Richmond.

SPM5   Defense Supply Center, Philadelphia.

SPM7   Defense Supply Center, Columbus.

SPM8   Defense Supply Center, Philadelphia—Construction & Equipment.

This is followed by the last two digits of the fiscal year in which the number was assigned.

A "T" in the ninth position of a solicitation number indicates that the RFQ was generated by an automated system. Once inventory of a particular item reaches a predetermined minimum level, the agency's computer will automatically generate a purchase request. These are eligible for award under the automated Procurement Automated Contract Evaluation (PACE) system.

Automated Awards — PACE

The Procurement Automated Contract Evaluation (PACE) program is an automated system that evaluates bids and makes an award electronically. The program uses pricing and other automated filters to make fully automated awards valued at $100,000 or less.

The solicitation is issued, offers are evaluated, and contracts are awarded electronically. The PACE system will only consider "qualified quotes" for an award; the quotes must be in *exact* compliance with the requirements stated in the solicitation, and must be submitted via the agency's Defense Internet Bid Board System (DIBBS).

PACE evaluates all qualified quotes on the basis of price alone and does not consider quantity price breaks. In the event of a tie between qualified quotes, the award will be based on the following order of precedence:

1. A domestic end product offer over a non-qualifying country end product offer.
2. A small business offer over a large business offer.
3. An offer with the shortest delivery period.
4. The first quote submitted.

Manual Awards

If the PACE system cannot make price reasonableness or contractor responsibility determinations, then the quote will be evaluated and awarded manually. In this case the contracting officer may consider quantity price breaks offered without further solicitation or discussion. If the requirement is evaluated manually, then price, delivery, and past performance will be considered.

AUTO-IDPOS

Automated Indefinite Delivery Purchase Order (IDPO) is a part of the Defense Logistics Agency's e-Commerce system that creates Indefinite Delivery Indefinite Quantity (IDIQ) awards below the simplified acquisition threshold ($100,000). Auto-IDPO uses pricing logic and other automated filters to make fully automated IDPO awards. These awards do not specify a firm quantity of supplies other than a minimum quantity. Auto-IDPOs are awarded for a Base Year and one option year. You must submit your quote via the DIBBS Internet Bid Board System. Quotes received by mail, fax, or e-mail will *not* be considered for award.

Just like the PACE system, AutoIDPO will only consider "qualified quotes" for award. Qualified quotes submit pricing and delivery for *all* quantity ranges, destinations, and option years as solicited.

Bids Without Exception are quotes that submit pricing and delivery for all quantity ranges, destinations, and option years and are in exact compliance with the solicitation requirements—that is, they offer the exact product, the quote is valid for a minimum of 90 days, and they comply with the terms listed on the solicitation for packaging, FOB point, source inspection, and allowable quantity variance.

Alternate Bids offer an item other than the exact approved item cited in the procurement item description (PID).

Bids With Exception are those quotes that do not submit pricing and delivery for all quantity ranges, destinations, and option years as solicited. Alternatively they may be quotes that take exception to certain requirements for minimum quote valid days, packaging, inspection, or quantity variance. These will not be considered for automated award.

APPROVED PART NUMBERS AND ALTERNATE PART NUMBERS

If the solicitation lists an approved manufacturer, you must provide that manufacturer's part number. If you wish to supply your own part and be recognized as an approved source, you will have to submit your bid as an Alternate Offer/Bid. The PACE system will not consider an alternate offer for an award, but they may be submitted for acceptance for future procurements. For Indefinite Delivery Purchase Orders, you may bid an Alternate Product, and you must submit all technical data to the Buyer.

THE REFERENCES TAB

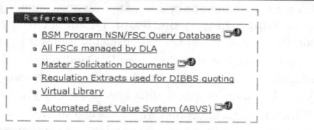

NSN/FSC QUERY DATABASE

Also known as WebFlis, this is a site where you can find out whether a particular National Stock Number (NSN), National Identification Number (the NSN minus the first 4 digits), or Part Number is included in the Business System Modernization (BSM) Program.

ALL FSCS MANAGED BY DLA

You can also find out which Federal Supply Codes (FSCs) are managed by the Defense Logistics Agency.

MASTER SOLICITATION DOCUMENT

Download this very important document, as it gives exact details of the regulations that apply to the contract, terms and conditions, and so on. This document is used for Request for Quotes (RFQs) and Purchase Orders for automated Business System Modernization (BSM) acquisitions valued up to $100,000 for each of the Defense Supply Centers (Columbus, Philadelphia, and Richmond). You will need to read the document carefully in order to understand the solicitation, evaluation, and award process. Each provision is provided in full text in Part I of the Master Solicitation.

The Master Solicitation document is updated from time to time to reflect changes to regulations or acquisition policies. Do not assume, once you have downloaded a copy, that it will remain effective. Updates are identified by a date and revision number, and changes are highlighted in each revision.

Part I contains important information about this document, the Internet Bid Board System, and the Procurement Automated Contract Evaluation (PACE) system.

Part II contains information about Indefinite Delivery Purchase Order (IDPO) contracts, which do not specify a firm quantity of supplies, other than a minimum quantity. In these cases, delivery orders will be issued during the period of the contract.

Part III contains the clauses, provisions, or notices that apply to automated solicitations and orders. Web links are provided to the Federal Acquisition Regulations (FAR) as well as to the Defense Federal Acquisition Supplement (DFARS) and others. Each Center's clause list is also provided. If clauses, provisions, or notices are incorporated by reference, and the full text is not provided, they have the same force and effect as if they were given in full.

THE AUTOMATED BEST VALUE SYSTEM

This is a computerized system that collects information on how well a vendor has fulfilled the terms of any previous contracts, and converts that into a numeric score. The contracting officer will use this information as an additional evaluation factor when making Best Value Award decisions. (See Chapter 2 for more details about this system.)

The Technical Data Tab

Drawings and Technical Documents

 When you click on any solicitation notice, you may come across links to drawings or technical documents that are available for download and viewing.

cFolders—New in 2006. Technical data is now available at the Defense Logistics Agency's new Collaboration Folders (cFolders) Website. This site contains Bidsets, Engineering Data Lists, and digitized drawings for open BSM-DIBBS procurements. You will need to have an active DIBBS account to access this site.

Restricted Drawings. Certain drawings may be restricted. In order to access restricted drawings, you must complete form DD 2345, the U.S./Canada Joint Certification Program (JCP). The drawings will only be made available to the person who is designated as the Data Custodian for your company. No access will be given to certain restricted drawings, or to any restricted drawing that contains limited/proprietary data. However, it will provide index information and an order form for CDs for these drawings. Drawings that are not in electronic format, are classified, or have restrictions on dissemination may be ordered by clicking on "Manual Request."

Drawing Distribution Codes:

Code A—Unrestricted.

Code X—Export Controlled.

Code C—Government Agencies and contractors only.

Code D—DOD and DOD contractors only.

Icon	File Type	File Extension	Download Web Site
	Adobe® Acrobat	PDF	http://www.adobe.com/products/acrobat/readstep.html
	Microsoft® Word	DOC	http://office.microsoft.com/Assistance/9798/viewerscvt.aspx
	Microsoft® Excel	XLS	http://office.microsoft.com/Assistance/9798/viewerscvt.aspx
	Microsoft® PowerPoint	PPT	http://office.microsoft.com/Assistance/9798/viewerscvt.aspx
	Compressed/Archive	ZIP	http://www.pkware.com or http://www.winzip.com
	CALS Raster	C4	http://jtshelp.redstone.army.mil

Viewing Drawings

Document Level - Listing All Documents and Sheets

Doc Num	Cage Code	Doc Type	Doc Rev	Sheet Num	Sheet Rev	Sub Sht	Frm Num	Acc	File Type	File Ext
12579607	19200	DR	B	001	B		0001		1	C4
6650448	53711	DR	C	001	C		0001		1	C4
6650448	53711	QS	B	001	B		0001		1	C4
6650448	53711	QS	B	002	B		0001		1	C4
6650448	53711	QS	B	003	B		0001		1	C4
							# Documents = 5			

This is a typical drawing list.

Drawings are in various formats. You will first need to download specific viewer software in order to view these drawings.

As you can see, there are five documents in all.

The table shows the manufacturer's Commercial and Government Entity (CAGE) Codes and Document types. DR refers to Drawings—in this instance the first DR document lists Tolerance Tables, and the second shows the Source drawing. Document Type QS is used for the Quality Assurance Provisions. The Revision numbers are listed, as well as the File Type and File Extension. The .c4 file extension refers to ImageR viewing software, which is often used for drawings.

Still Can't Find What You Are Looking For?

If the drawings you are looking for do not seem to be available, you might begin by checking whether the solicitation is a Request for Proposal (RFP) or a Long Term Contract. (You can tell this by looking for an "R" in the ninth position of the solicitation number.)

The Defense Supply Center in Richmond has drawings and TDP data for their Request for Proposals at their Website: *https://ric1s-c025.dscr.dla.mil/tdmd/*.

The Defense Supply Centers in Philadelphia and Columbus will supply the information on a CD by e-mail request.

DSCC: CDDWGS@dscc.dla.mil

DSCP: dscpdrawings@dla.mil

If you are still unable to find the information, then you can e-mail or call the DIBBS helpdesk.

OTHER WEBSITES FOR OBTAINING DRAWINGS

The Acquisition Streamlining and Standardization Information System (ASSIST) allows you access to DOD-wide standardization documents. *http://assist.daps.dla.mil/online/start/*

The Defense Supply Center Philadelphia (DSCP) drawings site, known as AbiWeb, was retired in 2006.

DSCP solicitations beginning with "SP05" can be obtained by e-mailing dscpdrawings@dla.mil.

Drawings for solicitations starting with "SPM" or "SPE" are available at *https://dbi.dscc.dla.mil.*

The Military Engineering Data Asset Locator System, known as MEDALS, is the central index of engineering data for the Department of Defense.

www.dlis.dla.mil/medals

PROCUREMENT HISTORY

In many cases, the solicitation document will also contain information on past procurement—that is, which companies have supplied this item in the past, and their unit price. This is invaluable information for you to have *before* you submit your offer!

Here is an example of procurement history embedded on the second page of the solicitation document:

```
PROCUREMENT HISTORY FOR NSN: 3040004841448

STOCK BUYS:
TYPE  CAGE     CONTRACT NUMBER      QUANTITY     UNIT COST    AWD DATE
STK   98247    N0038301G035MYM56    000006       3890.70000   07/28/06
STK   98247    N0038301G035MYM84    000014       3890.70000   10/11/06
STK   1Y1P4    SP074005V1835        000006       3495.00000   11/26/04
STK   1Y1P4    SP074005D5L730001    000002       3495.00000   03/13/05
STK   1Y1P4    SP074004VC086        000010       3595.00000   06/14/04
```

As you can see, the item is identified first by using its National Stock Number (NSN).

In the first column you will either see the letters STK, indicating a Stock Buy, or DVD indicating a Direct Vendor Buy.

The second column shows you the company that supplied the item, using their Commercial and Government Entity (CAGE) code. Use the Business Identification Website to identify the company. Remember that if a company has more than one location or division it will have separate CAGE codes for each location.

www.bpn.gov

The third column lists the exact contract number that was awarded. If you wish, you may enter that number in the Awards tab on the DIBBS homepage and view the complete contract.

Column Four shows you the quantity that was ordered.

Column Five gives you the Unit Cost.

Column Six lists the date the contract was awarded.

At other times this same information can be found on the final page of the solicitation document, in a slightly different format.

OTHER IMPORTANT PROGRAMS

THE QUALITY SHELF LIFE PROGRAM

Certain items that can deteriorate through time need special handling. The Defense Logistics Agency's Quality Shelf Life Program controls those items in order to ensure that when they are procured they are within appropriate shelf-life dates.

These products include products such as rubber hoses, nuclear, biological and chemical items, ammunition and explosives, batteries, petroleum, oil and lubricants, packaging material, and hazardous wastes.

www.shelflife.hq.dla.mil/policy_documents.asp

ENVIRONMENTAL "GREEN" PURCHASING PROGRAMS

 The Defense Logistics Agency's Green Procurement Program encourages the purchase of products that have a lesser or reduced effect on human health and the environment, compared to other similar products. The DLA then assigns Environmental Attribute Codes (EACs) to these items.

APPROVED ENVIRONMENTAL ATTRIBUTES

Asbestos Alternative Products

Energy Efficient Products: For example, commercial appliances, heating ventilations and air conditioning (HVAC) equipment and residential windows, industrial centrifugal pumping systems, distribution transformers, and electric motors. Also applies to fluorescent lighting, computers, copiers, and fax machines.

Low Standby Power Products: Audio, TVs and DVDs, computer monitors and workstations, and major appliances such as microwave ovens.

Low Volatile Organic Compound (VOC) Products: Coatings, and household and cleaning products.

Recycled Content Products: Building insulation, carpets, cements and concretes; landscaping products, office products and paper; park and recreation products; and vehicular products such as coolants, oils, vehicle parts, and tires.

Water Conserving Products: Faucets, showerheads, and urinals.

If you feel that your product meets any of these "green" criteria you can register that information at the site. If your product meets the requirements, it will be tagged with a Green Product code and a Green Tree symbol in the Department of Defense Catalogs. For more information see the Website at *www.dlis.dla.mil/green/default.asp.*

OTHER "GREEN" PROGRAMS

The Federal Energy Management Program
www1.eere.energy.gov/femp/
Department of Energy
Selling energy-efficient products to the federal government
www1.eere.energy.gov/femp/pdfs/sell_to_gov.pdf
Environmental Protection Agency
Comprehensive Procurement Guidelines for Products
www.epa.gov/cpg/products.htm
Consolidated Recovered Materials Advisory Notice (RMAN)
EPA 530-R-04-034
www.epa.gov/fedrgstr/EPA-WASTE/1997/November/Day-13/f29733.htm
Environmental Technologies Opportunities Portal (ETOP)
www.epa.gov/etop/
Environmentally Preferable Purchasing
www.epa.gov/epp/
Building for Environmental & Economic Sustainability (BEES)
www.epa.gov/epp/tools/bees.htm
Department of Agriculture
Federal Biobased Products Preferred Procurement Program (FB4P)
www.biobased.oce.usda.gov/fb4p/

General Services Administration

GSA Environmental Products & Services Guide

www.fss.gsa.gov/enviro

Federal Procurement Opportunities for Green Vendors

www.ofee.gov/gp/GreenVendors_ReadSprd.pdf

QUOTING IN DIBBS

You must be registered and logged into DIBBS in order to submit quotes on RFQ solicitations.

Once you have found a solicitation that you would like to quote for, find your Solicitation via the RFQ Search and then click on the "Quote" icon displayed next to the solicitation number.

Click on the Solicitation # to view the RFQ & NSN/Part No. to view additional info.

#	NSN/Part No. Nomenclature	Technical Documents Bidset/Drawings	Spec/Stnd	Solicitation #	Auction Status	PR # PR QTY	Issue	Return By
1	1620-00-284-1298 SUPPORT, SHOCK STRUT - Mil-Spec	Tech Docs *Spec/Stnd Only*		SPM400-06-Q-0027 *Quote*		0012306947 QTY: 1	8/17/2006	09/15/2006
2	2925-00-102-6835 BAFFLEASSEMBLY, AIR Mil-Spec	Tech Docs		SPM407-06-T-0005 *Quote*		0012307574 QTY: 1	9/14/2006	09/28/2006
3	4710-01-271-2000 PIPE, PLASTIC	Avail	None	SPM700-05-T-B010 *Quote* SB		0011243586 QTY: 248	4/25/2005	05/09/2005
4	4710-01-353-9694 TUBE, METALLIC Mil-Spec	None	Avail	SPM700-05-T-9887 *Quote* SB		0011235562 QTY: 325	4/21/2005	05/05/2005

Once you have completed the form, make doubly sure that the information is accurate, and then click on "Submit." You will receive a message that your submission was "Successful" You may want to print a copy of the page that says your quote was successfully submitted for your records.

You may review your submitted quote any time until the requirement is either awarded or cancelled, and you will be able to revise your quote if you wish.

You may withdraw a quote by submitting a revised quote and choosing "No-Bid" under the drop-down menu for Bid Type. Make sure to click the "Submit" button again, to check that you receive the message that your new submission was successful.

Late Quotes: The solicitation return date/time is not a firm closing date on Request for Quotes, except for auctions. Quotes received after the return date/time will continue to run through the automated award process until the award process has begun. Once the award process has begun (on the closing date), late quotes will only be considered if the Contracting Officer determines that it is in the best interests of the Government and that accepting the late quote would not unduly delay the award.

Auctions: Be aware that if you see a gavel icon on the RFQ search results page, or on the Web quote form, then the requirement is an auction candidate. By submitting a quote on an auction solicitation you agree that your quoted price, and other price-related factors, may be publicly displayed. Bidders remain anonymous. If you wish to view open auctions you must be logged in to the secure portion of DIBBS.

STEP-BY-STEP THROUGH YOUR ONLINE QUOTE IN DIBBS

This section takes you step-by-step through the Defense Internet Bid Board System (DIBBS) online quoting system, and shows you exactly how to complete the form and submit your offer.

Solicitation #	Enter the Solicitation number here.
Login CAGE	Enter the Commercial and Government Entity (CAGE) code of the user who is registered in DIBBS.
Quoting For CAGE	You may register yourself as an authorized representative who can submit bids on behalf of another company. If this is the case, enter the CAGE code of the company who will receive the award; otherwise leave this section blank.

Buyer Code	Enter the buyer code here.
Bid Type	**Bid Without Exception.** Your quote is in exact compliance with the solicitation requirements. **Bid With Exception.** There are exceptions to the solicitation requirements. For example: exceptions to packaging requirements; to FOB point; quoting destination inspection when the solicitation requires origin inspection; exceptions to the solicited quantity; quoting a quantity variance when not allowed by the solicitation, or seeking exceptions to the quantity variance that is allowed by a solicitation. **Alternate Bid.** This indicates that a substitute product is being offered, or that there are other variations from the item description. **No Bid.** This indicates that you do not wish to bid. For example, if you wish to withdraw a previous bid before the due date for offers has passed, you may use this option to do so. Quoting a zero quantity for all line items will force a bid type of "No Bid."
Discount Terms	Select from pick list of the six most common discount terms.
Vendor Quote #	This is an optional fill-in for your reference only.
Quote Valid For	State the number of days that your quote will remain valid.
Meets Packaging and RFID Requirements	**Compliance With DFARS 252.211-7006 is Mandatory.- NEW!** Beginning October 1, 2006, the <u>only</u> acceptable tags are EPC Class 1 passive RFID tags that meet the EPC global Class 1 Generation 2 specification. Class 0 and Class 1 Generation 1 tags will no longer be accepted after September 30, 2006. You must affix passive RFID tags, at the case and palletized unit load packaging levels. **NEW!** After December 2006, this question will no longer default to Yes in this online quoting form—you must complete this mandatory question. For more information, read the complete DFARS clause: DFARS 252.211-7006 Radio Frequency Identification.

Federal Supply Schedule (FSS)-Basic Ordering Agreement (BOA) Blanket Purchase Agreement (BPA)	If you have a Federal Supply Schedule contract number (also known as a GSA contract), a Basic Ordering Agreement, or a Blanket Purchase Agreement Number, you must enter it here, along with the expiration date.
Free On Board (FOB) Point	Also sometimes known as Freight On Board. **FOB Origin:** The agency is responsible for freight charges. **FOB Destination:** You are responsible for freight charges.
Govt. Inspection Point	For Origin Inspection, supply the CAGE code where you want the Government to inspect the supplies—either at your facility (enter your CAGE code), or at the manufacturer's plant (enter their CAGE code). **Packaging CAGE code:** If you want inspection at your facility or plant, use your CAGE code. If it is at a packaging house, use their CAGE code.
SPI Process Proposed	The Single Process Initiative (SPI) is a DOD program where you may propose an alternate management or manufacturing process in lieu of a specific military or Federal specification or standard. If you have a process that has already been approved under this program, you would enter that number here. For details see DFARS 252.211-7005.
Price and Delivery Data Area	
Price & Delivery (Non-Indefinite Delivery Contract)	Enter your price, and your delivery, in number of days ADO (After Date of Order).
Minimum Order Quantity	Enter your minimum order quantity here.
Quantity Variance	Enter any variation in the quantity that you propose, compared to the quantity requested in the solicitation document.In the solicitation document you will find a section where an allowable percentage variance is listed.

Quantity Available for Immediate Shipment	Is there a quantity available for immediate shipment? If so, enter the quantity, price, and number of delivery days.
Price Break Ranges	Enter price break ranges and unit prices here.
Pricing & Delivery Indefinite Delivery Purchase Order	Enter quantities and pricing for specific quantities. For example you may wish to quote one price for a quantity range from 1–10; and another price on a quantity from 11–50. Enter the prices and ranges here.
Indefinite Delivery Purchase Order Alternate Price Break Ranges	An Indefinite Purchase Order does not specify a firm quantity, only a minimum quantity. Delivery Orders will be issued during the term of the contract. You must submit prices and delivery times for all the quantity ranges, geographical zones, and option years that have been solicited.
Quantity Variance	Enter any variation in the quantity that you propose, compared to the quantity requested in the solicitation document.In the solicitation document you will find a section where an allowable percentage variance is listed.
Product Offered Representations Data Area	
Supplies Offered	Are the items offered: In accordance with the cited specifications, standards, or drawings? Based on a different revision of these specifications, standards, and drawings? Based on changes to the cited specifications, standards, or drawings? Based on other technical data? Is there an error in the item description?
Part Number Offered	When an Approved manufacturing source or sources is specified, you may elect to offer an Exact item, an Alternate item, or a Reverse-Engineered Product. An Exact Product means the identical product described by the approved manufacturer's CAGE and part number. It is either manufactured by, under the direction of, or under agreement with the specified manufacturer. Any other product is considered

	an Alternate Product, even if it is manufactured in accordance with the drawings and/or specifications of the approved manufacturer.If you are offering an Alternate Product, enter the CAGE and part number offered.
Qualification Requirements	If an item is listed on the Qualified Products List, enter the manufacturer's CAGE, the Source's CAGE (if known), the Item Name, Service ID, and Test Document Number. For more details see FAR 52.209-1
Manufacturer or Dealer	State whether you are the Manufacturer; Dealer; Qualified Supplier List Manufacturer or Qualified Supplier List Dealer.
Higher Level Quality	If a higher-level quality standard/system is required you must select the standard/system that applies. If you select "other equivalent system" you must enter a description. See (FAR 46.202-4).
Material Requirements	Identify whether the item offered is used, reconditioned, remanufactured, or new/unused government surplus.
Hazardous Material Identification and Material Safety Data	If these documents are required, you must list them here. See DFARS 252.223-7001.
Buy American Act Balance of Payments Program Certification	Is the item being offered: A Domestic End Product?A Qualifying Country End Product? (choose from the list of countries)A Non-qualifying Country End Product? (List the country, if known.)
Buy American ActNorth American Free Trade Agreement Implementation Act Balance of Payments Program Certification	Domestic End Product? Qualifying Country End Product?- Free Trade Agreement Country End Product? Other Foreign End Product?

Duty Free Entry Requested	Select "yes" if duty free entry is requested. Are the foreign supplies now in the United States? Has the duty been paid?- What amount is included in the offer to cover such duty?
Certification Regarding Knowledge of Child Labor for Listed End Products	Are you providing an end product that may have been mined, produced, or manufactured by forced or indentured child labor? This list currently includes items from Burma and Pakistan, including Bamboo, Beans, Bricks, Chilies, Corn, Pineapples, Rice, Rubber, Shrimp, Sugarcane, and Teak. The Dept Labor's current list of these products and corresponding countries is at *www.dol.gov/ILAB/regs/eo13126/main.htm*.
Contractor Representations Data Area	
Taxpayer Identification Number (TIN)	Enter your Taxpayer Identification Number, and choose the Organization Type.
Small Business and Other Business Type Representations	Are you A Small Business? A JWOD Participating Non-profit Agency? An Historically Black College/University or other Minority Institution? An Educational Institution? An Intragovernmental Institution? A Large Business? If you are a Small Business, are you a small disadvantaged business? A woman-owned small business? A veteran-owned or service-disabled veteran-owned small business? A business located in a HUB-Zone?
Affirmative Action Compliance	Select from a list of representations regarding affirmative action programs. See FAR 52.222-25 and FAR 52.212-3(d)(3).
Previous Contracts and Compliance Reports	Select from a list of representations regarding previous contracts and compliance reports. See FAR 52.222-22 and FAR 52.212-3(d)(3).
Alternate Disputes Resolution	Do you agree to use alternate dispute resolution? See DLAD 52.233-9001.

Remarks	You may add remarks here, except for bids that are eligible for Automated (PACE) awards. PACE awards are identified by a "T" or a "U" in the ninth position of the solicitation number.

BATCH QUOTING

Batch Quoting is a faster way for you to submit bids for multiple Request for Quotes (RFQs). You can prepare up to 75 lines at a time, using a pre-set format. Once you have them all ready, you can then upload all the quotes to DIBBS at one time.

BSM DIBBS Batch File Format:

www.dibbs.bsm.dla.mil/Refs/help/BatchFileFormat.htm

Sample preformatted RFQ Batch Download Files for BSM DIBBS:

www.dibbs.bsm.dla.mil/Refs/help/bqSample.zip

A Microsoft Access 2000© database file is available to help you to create your file, using the correct format for upload:

www.dibbs.bsm.dla.mil/Refs/help/BatchQuoteFileImport ExportDirections.pdf

FINDING INFORMATION ON AWARDS

Once an award has been made, you may access it from the homepage link. You can search for a specific award using the National Stock Number (NSN), the item's nomenclature, the manufacturer using the Commercial and Government Entity (CAGE) code, the part number, and so on.

Click on the Contract # to view the Award Document or Package.

#	Contract #	Delivery Order#	Awardee CAGE	Award Date	Total Contract Price	NSN/ Nomenclature	PR # or Req # / Solicitation	Award Posted
1	N0038301G015N	YMG1	78286	9/6/2005	$9,958.37	5998013314045 PRINTED WIRING BOARD	0011556661 SPM70005TW302	9/6/2005
2	N0038302G003H	Y8E5	59211	5/9/2006	$1,001.19	5998010634667 PRINTED WIRING BOARD	0012095294 SPM7A206T0307	5/9/2006
3	N0038304G018F	Y811	072E5	3/9/2006	$18,855.00	5998015257452 PRINTED WIRING BOARD	0012068232 SPM7M806Q0168	3/9/2006

This is very useful information for future research, even if you do not win the contract yourself. As you can see, you can find out who won the contract, and the total contract price.

Sometimes the company that was awarded the contract did not necessarily offer the lowest price. If the award was made using the Procurement Automated Contract Evaluation (PACE) automated program, then a bid that did not conform exactly to the stated requirements will not be considered, even if it is the lowest bid. Perhaps they did not bid on the exact product, or did not conform to packaging or marking requirements.

Icons Used in DIBBS

Icon	Narrative
Quote	Quote. By clicking on this icon, you can quote on a solicitation.
✓	Quote Submitted. A quote has been submitted for this solicitation. Clicking it take you to submitted quotes page.
▲	Revise Quote. Clicking this icon allows you to revise a your quote. The quote form will populate with previously entered data.
RC	Required Change. The solicitation requirements changed since you quoted. A new quote is required.
Q	There is a Submitted Quote (click to view).
Bwd	There is a bidset available for the NSN (click to access).
📖	There is a Specification or Standard available for download (click to access).
Mil-Spec	The NSN has an associated Military Specification.
QPL	The NSN has an associated Qualified Products Lists (QPL).
TD	There are Technical Documents available for the NSN (click to access).
HELP	Solicitation displayed may not include all pertinent data (click to obtain additional information)
⚡F	This is a Fast Award candidate. Quotes $2500 or less may be awarded prior to the solicitation return date (see DLA Master Solicitation for Automated Solicitations and Resulting Awards).
R	There is an RFQ document available (click to access).
Ipro	Automated Indefinite Delivery Purchase Order
SB	Solicitation is Small Business Set-Aside.
HUBZone	Solicitation is a HUBZone Set-Aside.
SDVOSB	Solicitation is a Service Disabled Veteran-Owned Small Business Set-Aside.
C Combined Set-Aside	Solicitation is a Combined Set-Aside.

CHAPTER 4

ADDITIONAL PROCUREMENT SITES

PROCUREMENT GATEWAY (PROGATE)

Until recently this was an important site for smaller procurement opportunities, up to a maximum of $25,000. However, in 2007, the Department of Defense moved many of the items normally purchased via this site to their Internet Bid Board System (DIBBS), which we discussed in the previous chapter. Opportunities still appear at this site, however, and you may wish to see if the products you can supply are still purchased through ProGate.

Procurement Gateway only posts sales opportunities for products, *not* services. Offers at this site are made electronically, through the Internet Quoting System.

The Procurement Gateway Website address is *http://progate.daps.dla.mil/home/*.

Along the side of the homepage you will see various options, including:

- Search.
  - **RFQ—Request for Quote.** This type of solicitation is issued when the value of the bid is estimated to be less than $100,000. In a Request for Quote (RFQ) document, the agency involved knows exactly what they are looking for, and they will be very specific in their description. The agency will notify you of the specific manufacturer and the part number required, along with any military specification numbers and/or drawing numbers.

  - **RFP—Request for Proposal.** In a Request for Proposal (RFP) document the government is looking for a product, but they are not aware of the different models and capabilities that may be available to them. They are asking you to propose a product. Unlike a Request for Quote, these Requests for Proposals are negotiable. Although price is always a factor in awards, it is not always the deciding factor. The deciding factor in a proposal is the one that is most advantageous to the government. This is known as Best Value Purchasing.

  - **Awards.** Any contracts that are awarded will be issued from this site. It is your responsibility to monitor this site for awards.

- Related Data.
  - **Drawings, Specifications, & Standards.** When drawings, specifications, or standards are available, they will be noted in the descriptive portion of the solicitation.

- **Quotes.** This section registers you with a User ID and Password, which allows you to submit offers electronically.

■ Other.

  - **User Profile.** The User Profile option allows registered users to create and customize searches against account-specific profiles. Profile-based searches locate data that is important to you!

  - **Collection Download.** This option allows you to search and collect files on Request for Quotes using Federal Supply Classification (FSC) codes.

  - **Related Links.** This section contains links to various sites that contain a lot of helpful information about getting started, Dun & Bradstreet numbers, Commercial & Government Entity (CAGE) codes, links to the Small Business Administration, Procurement Technical Assistance Centers in your area, Federal Regulations, and links to other government agencies.

YOUR SEARCH OPTIONS AT THIS SITE

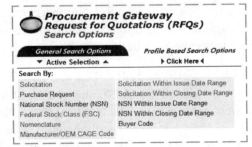

SEARCH BY SOLICITATION

If you would like to research the details of a specific solicitation, and you know the solicitation number, you would click on this tab. Enter the solicitation number here. Do not include any spaces or dashes.

Center: You may prefer to search all the agencies sites here, but if you wish, you may further limit your search by using the drop-down button on the Center tab. For example, the Defense Supply Center in Philadelphia (DSCP) handles quotes for General & Industrial supplies, as well as Clothing & Textiles. Other options here are the Defense Supply Center at Richmond (DSCR) or the Defense Supply Center in Columbus (DSCC).

Solicitation Type: You will probably prefer to leave the All Types option here. Solicitations Types are either known as Q-Quotes or T-Quotes.

A T-Solicitation is an RFQ that is valued at under $25,000. They are generated automatically by the system and are not created by a particular buyer. T-Solicitations are posted automatically to the Gateway every morning.

A Q-Solicitation is an RFQ that falls under Simplified Acquisition Procedures ($100,000). Q-Solicitations are created by a buyer, rather than generated automatically. They are issued in Portable Document Format (PDF) format. For more details on this, see the Federal Acquisitions Regulations Parts 12, 13, and 13.5 at *www.arnet.gov/far.*

SEARCH BY PURCHASE REQUEST

If you know the Purchase Request Number, you can search under this heading. The same options are available to you here as when you search using the Solicitation number.

SEARCH BY NATIONAL STOCK NUMBER

If you know the National Stock Number (NSN) of the product you wish to search, enter it here. The National Stock Number is a number given to an item that is repeatedly bought, stocked, stored, issued, and used throughout the federal supply system. The NSN is 13 digits long; the first four digits represent the Federal Stock Class

(FSC), which we spoke about previously: In Chapter 1 we reviewed the National Stock Number (NSN) being 13 digits long; the first four digits represent the Federal Stock Class (FSC).

In many instances additional descriptive data is assembled that is known as a Product Item Description, or PID. The PID includes information such as price, item name, manufacturer's part number, and physical and performance characteristics.

SEARCH BY FEDERAL STOCK CLASS

This four-digit numerical system identifies specific categories of products. We spoke about identifying your product's FSC class in Chapter 1.

SEARCH BY NOMENCLATURE

When you first begin searching this site on your own, this is the heading that will search for a product category, and allow you to find the solicitations in your product line.

SEARCH USING MANUFACTURER/OEM CODE

This is where to search if you know the manufacturer's part number that you want to supply, or you know the manufacturer's Commercial and Government Entity (CAGE) code. There is a more detailed discussion of CAGE codes in Chapter 1.

If you are a dealer who can supply products from a particular manufacturer, then this is a great way to begin searching!

SEARCH USING AN ISSUE DATE RANGE OR A CLOSING DATE RANGE

These options allow you to search for solicitations that have been issued within a specific range of dates, or that have a range of specific closing dates. For example, you may wish to find all the solicitations that have been issued between January 1st and January 15th, or for solicitations with closing dates between January 1st and January 15th.

SEARCH FOR A NATIONAL STOCK NUMBER (NSN) USING AN ISSUE DATE RANGE OR A CLOSING DATE RANGE

In some instances you may only have the National Stock Number available to you. This is enough information to allow you to be made aware of open solicitations for that product within a certain date range. For example, you may wish to find all the solicitations that have been posted between January 1st and January 15th; or perhaps search for solicitations with closing dates between June 15th and June 30th.

SEARCH BY BUYER CODE

Every individual buyer has a code, and each buyer purchases a certain range of products. The buyer's name, code, and phone number can be found on the first page of the solicitation. Alternatively, you can search for a specific Request for Quote (RFQ) and then, on the results page, you can click on the National Stock Number link. If the solicitation comes from the Philadelphia office the buyer's name, code, and phone and fax numbers will be listed here. You can also search for a particular buyer's code at the appropriate DLA Website.

Defense Supply Center Philadelphia, General & Industrial:
http://saso.dscp.dla.mil/bidboard/buyloc.html

Defense Supply Center, Columbus:
https://dibbs.dscc.dla.mil/Buyer/

Procurement Gateway
Request for Quotations (RFQs)
Search Results - Nomenclature

Notice: Users that are having trouble viewing PDF-based documents may be experiencing a configuration problem related to the Adobe Reader plug-in. Please click here to access instructions on the Adobe Web site for reconfiguring the Adobe Reader as a helper application.

1 2 >

Go To Botto

#	Quoting	Drawings	Specs/ Stds	Solicitation # Purchase Request	NSN	Issue Date Closing Date	Item Description Quantity/Unit Issue
1				SP040004TLV92 YP004219000125	3110000701915	16-Feb-2005 24-Feb-2005	BEARING,BALL,ANNULAR 14 / EA
2				SP040005TP949 YP005046000104	3120014746441E	16-Feb-2005 03-Mar-2005	BEARING,SLEEVE
3				SP040005TP950 YP005046000105	3120007224251	16-Feb-2005 03-Mar-2005	BEARING, SLEEVE /
4				SP040005TP951 YP005046000108	3130013004302	16-Feb-2005 03-Mar-2005	BEARING,LINER,HOUSING /
5				SP040005TP954 YP005046000109	3110011294154	16-Feb-2005 03-Mar-2005	SEAT,BEARING /

THE SEARCH RESULTS

 Quoting: In the first block you can see the letters IQS. This indicates the Internet Quoting System. If this icon appears, you will be able to submit your offer electronically.

Drawings: If drawings are available for this solicitation, you would see a small pencil icon in this column. Clicking on the icon would allow you to download any available drawings.

Specs/Stds: If Specifications and/or Standards existed for this item, you would see a small paper icon in this column. Clicking on the icon would allow you to download these items.

In the Item Description column on the right-hand side you can see the items description, followed by the quantity required and the Unit of Issue. Where no specific quantity is listed, or where the quantity is listed as 1 or 0, a long-term indefinite-quantity contract may be indicated. Once you have found a solicitation for a product that you can supply, you can click on the link to find out more about this opportunity.

National Stock Number: Clicking on the NSN (National Stock Number) link can often give you more valuable information, such as a product description, specifications, and past procurement history

How to Obtain Drawings

If the solicitation that you are looking at contains a pencil icon, you can click here to obtain drawings. However, in order to view these drawings you will need to first download and install a specialized viewer onto your computer. The government provides two viewers—ImageR and JViewer—that are available at no cost to you.

Once you click on the Drawing icon, this information appears on your screen:

	Center= All, **Solicitation**= SP050006T8396, **NSN**= 5310013963874				
	The digitized drawings are in TILE RASTER CCITT Group 4 Compressed (JEDMICS C4) format. A viewer program that supports this format is required to display the drawing image.				
CAGE Code	Drawing Number	Drawing Type	Drawing Revision		Available Format
78286	70102-08010	DD	G		DIGITAL
78286	70102-08010	AL	T		DIGITAL
78286	70102-08010	AL	T		DIGITAL
78286	70102-08010	DA	G		DIGITAL
78286	70102-08010	DA	E		DIGITAL

Here you can see the Commercial & Government Entity (CAGE) code of the Manufacturer (78286), the Drawing Number, Drawing Type, Revision Number, and available format.

If you click on each link in the last column you will be able to download the drawings. (You may find that you have to save the item before you can view it, and change the file extension name. For example, if you use the ImageR viewer, it uses a ***.c4 file name)

OTHER SITES TO SEARCH FOR DRAWINGS

At the Defense Logistics Agency's Product Data Management Division (PDMD) Website you can find drawings using the NSN. Alternatively, you can use the Quicksearch option. You will need a user name and password to use this site:

https://ric1s-c025.dscr.dla.mil/tdmd/index.asp.

Some of the drawings in this Website are in file types other than c4 raster. For example some may be in the native CAD format, which would allow you to use the embedded engineering information in the drawing. Most of these formats will require different viewing packages to view the data. At the TDMD Website, you can click on the New Drawing Format link, to see other file types and viewer suggestions.

The Defense Supply Center Columbus has an Internet BidBoard System, where you can find military specifications and drawings.

https://dbi.dscc.dla.mil/

The DSCC/BSM also has a Bidset Interface site (DIBBS): *www.dibbs.bsm.dla.mil/.*

cFolders—New in 2006. In Chapter 3, we showed you how to retrieve drawings, specifications; and other technical data, now available via the Defense Logistics Agency's (DLA) new Collaboration Folders (cFolders) Website.

WHERE TO OBTAIN SPECIFICATIONS AND STANDARDS

Federal Specifications and Standards

http://apps.fss.gsa.gov/pub/fedspecs/index.cfm

Acquisition Streamlining and Standardization Information System (ASSIST): ASSIST Online offers Quicksearch which lets you search the ASSIST database for defense and federal standards,

Military Standards and handbooks, Qualified Products Lists, and so on. Non-Government Standards (NGS) are also available from ASSIST database—often for purchase via a credit card. *http://assist.daps.dla.mil*

National Standards System Network: Contains references to standards from more than 600 national and international developers, including the Department of Defense. You can search by document number or keywords in title or description. *www.nssn.org*

American National Standards Institute (ANSI): The ANSI Electronic Standards Store contains the complete ISO published standards. *www.ansi.org/*

CREATING A CUSTOM PROCUREMENT GATEWAY PROFILE

You must have a User Profile ID and Password in order to submit quotes via the Internet Quoting System (IQS). This option also allows you to create custom profiles based on specific National Stock Numbers (NSN) or Federal Supply Classifications (FSC). Once you have set up your custom profile you will receive notices via e-mail of any relevant Request for Quotes (RFQ). You will also be able to receive notices of any modifications or amendments. This system will also be used to notify you when you win an award.

TO SET UP YOUR PROFILE

At the left sidebar of the ProGate homepage, click on the User Profile option. Click on the keyboard icon to set up your profile. You will need to list your company's name, address, telephone, e-mail address, and so on, and you will also need your company's Commercial & Government Entity (CAGE) code.

You will then be able to select a single Federal Stock Class (FSC) that you would like to add to your profile, and click Submit. You can continue adding FSCs to your profile, one at a time, and submitting them.

Once you have chosen all your FSCs, click Continue Profile Setup. Now you will be able to add National Stock Numbers (NSNs) to your profile, if you wish.

Click the Finished button.

Request for Proposal (RFP) and Invitation for Bid (IFB) Notification. If you would like notification of these larger bids, select this option.

Click the Finished button.

A User ID and Password will be e-mailed to you. Keep it safe!

ARMY SINGLE FACE TO INDUSTRY (ASFI)

https://acquisition.army.mil/asfi

At this site you can search for Contracting Opportunities separately from Combined Synopsis/Solicitations.

You can search for the Most Recently Posted opportunities or those that close today. You can search for a specific Solicitation Number, or you can narrow your search to a particular site. You can use either the North American Industrial Classification system (NAICS) code or the Federal Supply Classification (FSC) code to search, or if you prefer, you can perform a text search.

Once you have found an opportunity that is of interest, click on the Solicitation link to view more details.

At the bottom of this page are links to more details. These links can take different forms. Sometimes there is a link to an Attachment that contains the solicitation documents. At other times the solicitation details are found at another agency site. You can click on this link to in order to view the document. At other times the details you need can be found at the bottom of the screen under Clins, or Contract Line Item Numbers.

Message Clauses reference specific Defense Federal Acquisition Regulations Supplements (DFARS):

Reference Type	Reference Number	Reference Date
Defense Federal Acquisition Regulations (DFAR)	252.204-7000	12/01/1991
Defense Federal Acquisition Regulations (DFAR)	252.204-7003	04/01/1992
Defense Federal Acquisition Regulations (DFAR)	252.204-7004 Alt A	11/01/2003
Defense Federal Acquisition Regulations (DFAR)	252.211-7003	06/01/2005
Defense Federal Acquisition Regulations (DFAR)	252.212-7000	06/01/2005
Defense Federal Acquisition Regulations (DFAR)	252.212-7001 (Dev)	04/01/2007
Defense Federal Acquisition Regulations (DFAR)	252.223-7001	12/01/1991
Defense Federal Acquisition Regulations (DFAR)	252.225-7000	06/01/2005
Defense Federal Acquisition Regulations (DFAR)	252.225-7001	06/01/2005

Shipping details show the shipping terms and the delivery address for each line item.

Clin	Transportation Charges/FOB	Acceptance/Inspection	Delivery Date/Period of Performance	Quantity	Ship to POC/Phone Number	DoDAAC - Ship To Address
0001	PS-Paid by Seller/DEST	DEST / DEST	01/12/2008-	30	No Contacts Identified-	W52H1B - TACOM-ROCK ISLAND, TRANSPORTATION OFFICER BLDG 299, EAST END RECG DOOR 16A, ROCK ISLAND, IL, 61299-5000, US

The Department of Defense Activity Address Code (DODAAC) is a six-position code that identifies a particular unit or organization that can requisition and receive material.

THE UNITED STATES POSTAL SERVICE

Although you are not able to search for solicitation notices at this site, the United States Postal Service Website has an online Supplier Registration System where you can enter information about your company's products and services. This information is then made available to their buyers. *www.usps.com/purchasing*

In addition, you can register under the Postal Service's Unsolicited Proposal Program..

United States Postal Service Publication 131 discusses this program.

www.usps.com/purchasing/purchasingpubs/pubsmenu.htm

The Innovations at USPS program encourages companies to propose new business ideas and new technologies. You may submit your proposal online for evaluation.

www.usps.com/innovations/

The Veterans Administration

www.bos.oamm.va.gov/bosxweb.htm

Veterans Affairs (VA) Medical Centers purchase pharmaceuticals, medical and surgical supplies, perishable items, facility operation equipment, supplies and materials, maintenance and repair services for medical/scientific equipment, building construction, maintenance and repair services, prosthetic/orthopedic aids, and medical gases.

The National Acquisition Center uses the General Services Administrations (GSA) Federal Supply Schedules for its contract programs. It is responsible for items such as medical, dental, and surgical supplies and equipment, pharmaceuticals and chemicals, prosthetic and orthopedic aids, high-tech medical systems, clinical analyzers, cost-per-test, Prime Vendor Distribution programs, and healthcare-related services.

The VA Central Office purchases Automatic Data Processing systems and equipment, communications systems and equipment, medical center construction, Architect/Engineer services, grave markers, retail store supplies, restaurant supplies, telecommunications, and consulting services.

The Denver Acquisition and Logistics Center procures items such as hearing aids, accessories and repair parts, prosthetic socks, orthopedic items such as corsets, binders, and abdominal supports, and aids for the legally blind (canes, braille items, and so on).

The Medical Surgical Prime Vendor Program is mandatory for all VA Medical Centers and consists of six prime vendor contracts. Medical Centers pay these vendors a distribution fee plus the product price. The distribution fee covers the costs for managing and administering the program. *www1.va.gov/vastorenac/docs/medsurgmainpage.htm*

FEDERAL PRISON INDUSTRIES (UNICOR)

www.unicor.gov/fpi_contracting/

UNICOR purchases the raw materials that are used in the Federal Prison Industries factories, located in federal prisons around the country. They produce goods and services for sale to government agencies only.

There are several separate business groups within the Federal Prison Industries:

Clothing & Textiles	Clothing for law enforcement, medical, and military personnel, as well as for Federal institutions. Draperies; curtains, mattresses, bedding, linens; towels; screen-printed textiles.
Electronics	Task lighting systems, wire harness assemblies, circuit boards, electrical components & connectors, electrical cables.
Fleet Management & Vehicular Components	Re-manufactured & refurbished vehicle components, retrofit services for new vehicles.
Industrial Products	Dormitory & quarters furnishings, industrial racking catwalks, mezzanines & warehouse/office shelving; lockers & storage cabinets, safety & prescription eyewear; fencing; filtration products; awards & promotional gifts, license plates & signs, custom engraving and printing.
Office Furniture	Office furnishings & accessories; office seating; casegoods & training tables; office systems products; filing & storage products.
Recycling Activities	Electronic and other recycling.
Services	Distribution & order fulfillment; assembly, packing & services; document conversion; call center & help desk support; printing & creative design services; laundry services.

You can see an alphabetical listing of these products at: *www.unicor.gov/prodservices/prod_dir_schedule/alphalist.cfm.* This listing also indicates whether a particular item is:

- **Competitive:** The Federal Prison Industries will compete for business on the same terms as any private sector offer.
- **Mandatory:** Federal customers MUST give these procurements to the Federal Prison Industries, as long as the item is available in the required timeframe and at a competitive price.
- **Non-Mandatory:** The Federal Prison Industries has waived the mandatory source requirement for this item.

Remember that UNICOR is interested in purchasing the raw materials for the products made in the prison factories, *not* the finished item. For example, they will purchase the material and thread required to make clothing, *not* the actual finished garment.

Federal Bureau of Prisons

If you are interested in supplying a specific prison or local correctional institution with your products, you will need to contact the individual institutions directly. Each facility is responsible for buying the necessary supplies services and equipment they need. Solicitations for larger opportunities (more than $25,000) are posted to the FedBizOpps Website, but if you are interested in smaller opportunities then you will need to contact these local institutions directly.

You can search for local institutions at *www.bop.gov.*

UNITED STATES PATENT OFFICE

In fiscal year 2007 the Patent Office's procurement offices are planning to implement the Vendor Self Service (VSS) system.

You must register as an Interested Vendor at this site, in order to participate in future procurement opportunities for simplified acquisitions (those estimated to be valued at $100,000 or less). Procurements greater than $25,000 will still be advertised at the FedBizOpps Website, but you will need to be registered at this Patent Office site in order to submit a quote, and you will have to submit your quote via this new system.

www.uspto.gov

Use the Site Map option to locate the Office of Procurement Web page, and follow the links to Vendor Self Service.

SUB-CONTRACTING OPPORTUNITIES — SUBNET

At the Small Business Administrations' Sub-Net site you can find relevant sub-contracting opportunities for your small business.

http://web.sba.gov/subnet/search/dsp_search_option.cfm

http://web.sba.gov/subnet/search/index.cfm

At the SBA's Sub-Contracting Opportunities page you can link to each individual state and view a list of the companies that are looking for small business sub-contractors. When a large business receives a federal government contract valued at greater than $100,000 (or greater than $1 million in the case of the Construction industry) the company is required to provide a Small Business Sub-Contracting Plan with its offer. The Small Business Administration (SBA) can help you to market your company as a sub-contractor to these prime contractors.

The Government Printing Office

http://contractorconnect.gpo.gov/

If you are a small printing business (forms, pamphlets, envelopes, and so on) then this site is for you! At the Quick Quote online small purchase system, you can bid electronically for printing contracts valued at less than $100,000.

You will need to register at this site in order to submit quotes.

Market Information at the Federal Procurement Data Center

Another government site you can find information to help you with market research is the Federal Procurement Data Center, or FPDC.

The agency maintains a system which contains a wealth of statistical information about federal contracting. You can find detailed information on contracts greater than $25,000 and summary data on procurements of less than $25,000.

Through this Website you can identify who brought what, from whom, for how much, when, and where.

There is also information on subcontracts (through the Subcontracting Data Systems) as well as foreign sales (via the Foreign Trade Data System).

You will need to register at this site, and create a user name and password, in order to have access to the information.

The Website address is *www.fpds.gov.*

Additional Procurement Sites

Listed here are some of the other procurement sites that you may wish to search, if you are looking for sales opportunities estimated to be valued at $25,000 or less.

Defense Supply Center Philadelphia
www.dscp.dla.mil/vendor.htm
Defense Supply Center Richmond
www.dscr.dla.mil
National Aeronautics and Space Administration (NASA)
http://prod.nais.nasa.gov/cgi-bin/nais/nasaproc.cgi
Navy:(NECO)
www.neco.navy.mil/

A SAMPLING OF OTHER FEDERAL PROCUREMENT SITES

Dept. of Agriculture
Procurement: *www.usda.gov/procurement/*

Dept. of Commerce
Acquisition Management: *http://oam.ocs.doc.gov/CAS_industry.html*

Selling to the Dept of Commerce: *www.osec.doc.gov/osdbu/Selling_to_DOC.htm*

Dept. of Defense; Defense Logistics Agency
Defense Supply Center Philadelphia: *www.dscp.dla.mil/vendor.htm*

Defense Supply Center Richmond, Aviation Supply: *www.dscr.dla.mil/*

United States Air Force
Contracting Business Center: *www.safaq.hq.af.mil/contracting/public/business/*

United States Army
Army Single Face to Industry: *https://acquisition.army.mil/asfi/*
(See the beginning of this chapter for details of this site.)

United States Navy
Electronic Commerce Online(NECO): *www.neco.navy.mil/*

Dept. of Education
Grants & Contracts:*www.ed.gov/fund/landing.jhtml?src=rt*

Department of Energy

Industry Interactive Procurement System (IIPS)

http://e-center.doe.gov/iips/busopor.nsf/ViewMenu?ReadForm

Dept. of Health & Human Services

Acquisition Management: *www.hhs.gov/oamp/*

Dept. of Housing & Urban Development (HUD)

Cont.racting: *www.hud.gov/offices/cpo/index.cfm*

Dept. of the Interior

National Business Center: *http://ideasec.nbc.gov/j2ee/login.jsp*

Dept. of Justice

Procurement: *www.usdoj.gov/07business/07_5.html*

Dept. of Labor

Grant & Contract Information: *www.dol.gov/oasam/grants/main.htm*

Dept. of Transport

Business Opportunities: *www.dot.gov/ost/m60/busopven.htm*

Environmental Protection Agency

Acquisition Management: *www.epa.gov/oam/srpod*

National Aeronautics and Space Administration (NASA)

Procurement Sites: *http://prod.nais.nasa.gov/cgi-bin/nais/nasaproc.cgi*

The Federal Acquisition Jumpstation

This very important link provides information on many different acquisition sites

http://prod.nais.nasa.gov/pub/fedproc/home.html

CHAPTER 5

SUBMITTING YOUR HARD COPY OFFER USING FEDERAL STANDARD FORMS (SF18, SF1449, SF33)

AN OVERVIEW

In Chapter 3, we discussed the Electronic Quoting System in detail. These bids were for relatively small sales opportunities, up to a maximum of $25,000.

Line-by-Line through the Standard Forms: For larger sales opportunities (up to $100,000) you will need to complete a hard copy or paper document. But don't despair; in this chapter we take you, page-by-page, through the document, so that you can confidently complete one of these larger bids.

Remember: Much of the information you must provide for this offer will be the same for many other bids that you might submit in the future. Once you are familiar with these questions, you will realize that most of the work in completing your offer is in understanding exactly what the agency is requesting, and determining your price.

Step-by-Step Through the Pages: Once again, we take you step-by-step through the pages of the document. We point out which sections must be completed and where to find the exact details of what the government is looking for, as well as delivery details and terms and conditions. We also discuss Federal Acquisition Regulations, and clauses incorporated by reference and by full text.

The Uniform Contract Format

Federal government agencies use several different types of Standard Forms when making purchases:

- Standard Form 1449, Solicitation/Contract/Order for Commercial Items.
- Standard Form 33, Solicitation, Offer and Award.
- Standard Form 18, Request for Quotations.

These are the most commonly used forms, but you may come across others. In most cases the overall requirements will be the same, but there may be slight differences in the layout.

The document must be printed out and mailed to the appropriate agency, unless you have verbal or written permission to submit your offer by fax. The name, phone number, fax number, and e-mail address of the Contracting Officer will always appear on Page 1 of the document. You may contact the Contracting Officer and ask for permission to submit your offer by way of fax.

Keep in mind that you will be answering many of the same questions over and over again in each offer you submit. The main difference between each offer is a description of the product or the Statement of Work. Once you are familiar with these questions, you will realize that most of the work in completing your offer is in understanding exactly what the agency is requesting, and determining your price.

All agencies format their solicitation documents in a specific, consistent way. You should be able to find the information you need, even though you may not have seen a particular agency's forms previously. This is known as the Uniform Contract Format.

- Section A: Solicitation/Contract Form.
- Section B: Supplies or Services and Prices/Costs.
- Section C: Description/Specifications/Statement of Work.

- Section D: Packaging and Marking.
- Section E: Inspection and Acceptance.
- Section F: Deliveries or Performance.
- Section G: Contract Administration Data.
- Section H: Special Contract Requirements.
- Section I: Contract Clauses.
- Section J: List of Attachments.
- Section K: Representations, Certifications and Other Statements.
- Section L: Instructions, Conditions, and Notices.
- Section M: Evaluation Factors.

To better understand each section clearly and so you can feel confident when you submit your offer, let's review each section:

SECTION A:
SOLICITATION/CONTRACT FORM

SOLICITATION/CONTRACT/ORDER FOR COMMERCIAL ITEMS *OFFEROR TO COMPLETE BLOCKS 12, 17, 23, 24, AND 30*		1. REQUISITION NUMBER FAG36N7 I06R001			PAGE 1 OF 9
2. CONTRACT NO.	3. AWARD/EFFECTIVE DATE	4. ORDER NUMBER	5. SOLICITATION NUMBER FA5209-07-T-0228		6. SOLICITATION ISSUE DATE 26-Jul-2007
7. FOR SOLICITATION INFORMATION CALL:	a. NAME HIROSHI YOSHIKAWA		b. TELEPHONE NUMBER (No Collect Calls) 042-552-3011		8. OFFER DUE DATE/LOCAL TIME 10:00 A M 14 Aug 2007
9. ISSUED BY CODE FA5209 FA5209 - 374TH CONTRACTING SQUADRON UNIT 5228, BLDG 620, YOKOTA AB FUSSA-SHI, TOKYO 197-0001 JAPAN		10. THIS ACQUISITION IS [X] UNRESTRICTED ☐ SET ASIDE: % FOR ☐ SMALL BUSINESS ☐ HUBZONE SMALL BUSINESS ☐ 8(A)	11. DELIVERY FOR FOB DESTINATION UNLESS BLOCK IS MARKED ☐ SEE SCHEDULE		12. DISCOUNT TERMS
			13a. THIS CONTRACT IS A RATED ORDER UNDER DPAS (15 CFR 700)		
TEL: FAX:		NAICS: SIZE STANDARD:	13b. RATING		
			14. METHOD OF SOLICITATION [X] RFQ ☐ IFB ☐ RFP		

SF 1449: Page one of the solicitation document. You can see in this example that you only need to complete certain blocks on this first page of the document: Blocks 12, 17, 23, 24, and 30.

Other sections on this first page include the following information:

Block 5—The Solicitation Number. If you need to speak to the Contracting Officer concerning this bid, you will quote this number.

Blocks 6 and 8—The Date Issued and the Due Date for Offers. In many cases the time between the issue date and the offer date is 30 days, but this can vary. For example, if the need is particularly urgent.

Block 7a and 7b—The Contracting Officer's name and phone number.

Block 9—Issued By. This is the name of the Agency that issued the quote.

Block 10—Is this acquisition a Small Business Set-Aside? In this particular case it is unrestricted.

Block 11—Delivery is Freight on Board Destination (FOB). In most instances you will ship "F.O.B. Destination." This means you are paying freight, and must include freight in your Unit Delivered Price.

Block 12—Discount Terms. This is where you would give a discount for prompt payment. You do not need to give a discount, as the agency is required by law to pay you in 30 days! My advice is to insert "Net 30 days" here.

Block 13a and 13b—Rating. Department of Defense contracts may be assigned priority ratings using the Defense Priority Allocation System or DPAS. There are two levels of priority: DO and DX. DO rated orders take preference over unrated orders. DX rated orders take preference over both DO rated and unrated orders. In this particular case the solicitation is unrated.
http://www.ml.afrl.afmil/dpas/dpas-what.html
http://guidebook.dcma.mil/38 DPAS%20Guidebook.htm

Block 14—Indicates whether this acquisition is a Request for Quote (RFQ), a Request for Proposal

(RFP), or an Invitation for Bid (IFB). See Chapter 1 for a discussion of these terms.

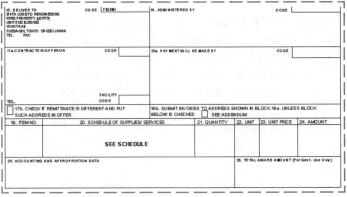

Block 15—The delivery address.

Block 16—For agency use.

Block 17a—Fill in your company's name, address, and telephone number here. Sometimes this section will also request your DUNS number. (See Chapter 1 for further information.)

Block 17b—Would you like payment to go to a different address from the one you listed in Block 17a? If so, check this box and include the remittance address in the offer.

Block 18—The agency that will make the payments to you.

Blocks 19 through 24—The details of the items required and the quantities requested will be listed later in the solicitation document.

Block 25—For agency use.

Block 26—The agency will fill in the amount here when the contract is awarded.

Block 27—Certain additional documents (in this case some Federal Acquisition Regulations) that you will need to read and understand are attached. Other attachments might include an amendment to the solicitation, or the specifications of the product.

Block 28—The number of copies of the solicitation you are required to submit. Make a note of this section, as your offer could be rejected if you do not comply with this request!

Block 29—This will be completed by the agency when the contract is awarded.

Block 30a, 30b, and 30c—The signature of the person authorized to sign the quote; the printed or typed name of that person, and the date of the signature.

Blocks 32 through 42—These sections are completed by the agency, and contain information on the acceptance and inspection of the product; the name and contact information of the government representative; and other details that need to be completed by the agency in order for them to authorize payment to you.

SECTION B:
SUPPLIES/SERVICES AND PRICES/COSTS

Here is an example of two slightly different versions of the next section, which details exactly what the agency is looking for, and the quantity requested.

ITEM NO	SUPPLIES/SERVICES	QUANTITY	UNIT	UNIT PRICE	AMOUNT
0001		1	Each		
	VEHICLE				
	FFP				
	VEHICLE TYPE: AMBULANCE MODULAR 4X2				
	See Attached Specification and Requirements				
	NSN: 2310-01-129-4702				
	NSN: 2310-01-129-4702				
	MILSTRIP: F4O3M37106A001				
	PURCHASE REQUEST NUMBER: F4O3M37106A001				
	SIGNAL CODE: A				
			NET AMT		

Page 2 of 12

SECTION B Supplies or Services and Prices

ITEM NO	SUPPLIES/SERVICES	QUANTITY	UNIT	UNIT PRICE	AMOUNT
0001		3.00	Each		
	Power Cables				
	FFP - Mfg: J & N Aviation, P/N JB8816-100SNJ or equal, 100 ft, ETL listed, 260 amp, 400HZ, single jacked double ended cable assembly 18 #18's (control), 6 #4's (phase) & 1 *1 for neutral. Molded strain relief behind heads and patened high visibility (yellow) r				
	NSN 6150-03-POW-CABL				
	MILSTRIP F44LGL31050200				
	PURCHASE REQUEST NUMBER F44LGL31050200				
	SIGNAL CODE A				
			NET AMT		

Item No. This column indicates that this is the first item requested in this bid package. If there was more than one item request in this solicitation, you would see Line Item #002 later in the solicitation, followed by the second item details. You may come across the term CLIN.

CLIN (Commodity Line Item Number). There may be only one line item or there may be several. The agency will use separate *line item numbers*, not only for requesting different products, but also when they are looking for just one item but need different quantities shipped to different locations, or with different delivery terms. For example, Line Item # 0001 may list a quantity of 50 and a delivery to California, while Line Item # 0002 may be for the same product, but with a quantity of 75, or a requested 3-day delivery time, or a delivery to a different location.

In many cases the purchasing agency will list a certain quantity on Line Item # 0001, and then list an option quantity of an additional number of units in Line Item #0002. The agency may choose whether or not to exercise this second option.

This subject is discussed in more detail in Chapter 2.

Supplies/Services. This section gives you a detailed description of the item they are requesting, including the type of pricing (FFP: Firm Fixed Price), the manufacturer, part number, and product specifications.

The term "or equal" means that you are permitted to offer a product that is equal to or better than the specified product. You will need to provide documentation about your equivalent product.

MILSTRIP, Purchase Request Number, and Signal Code are for government agency purposes only.

Quantity/Unit/Unit Price/Amount. These columns show you the total quantity requested, and the Unit (which is often "each," but could also be for example "dozen," "gallon," "gross," and so on). Be careful here to note the Unit of Issue. You don't want to quote for a single bottle if the Unit of Issue (U/I) requested is a 12-bottle case! The next column is where you write in your Unit Price. Remember that your Unit Price is a Unit Delivered Price.

Always include freight in your offer. In the final column you would insert the total cost of Line Item #0001.

A list of the two-digit Unit of Issue Codes can be found in the Appendices section of this book. If you are uncertain, check with the Contracting Officer before you submit your offer.

SECTION C:
DESCRIPTION/SPECIFICATIONS/
WORK STATEMENT

```
PURCHASE ORDER NUMBER 98500-7-1224
LEAD-BASED PAINT INSPECTIONS AND RISK ASSESSMENTS FOR
U.S. FISH AND WILDLIFE SERVICE
IN THE STATES OF
ALABAMA, INDIANA, IOWA, MINNESOTA, NORTH DAKOTA,
SOUTH CAROLINA, TENNESSEE, AND UTAH


I.      DESCRIPTION OF WORK

A.      Objective

(1) This delivery order consists of performing lead-based paint inspections and risk assessments in 20 Fish and Wildlife
Service (Service) owned residences and preparing an inspection/risk assessment report for each residence.  These residences
generally have 2 or 3 bedrooms, and may have basements.
```

Section C of the solicitation document gives you detailed descriptions of what the agency requires. Naturally, if the product you supply is relatively straightforward, there may not be a lot of additional information in this section. In this particular example, the solicitation is for a service contract, and this section gives a detailed description of the requirement. This is where you will find exactly what the agency is looking for!

For Service contracts, such as this example, Section C is several pages long and describes, in detail, the work required, the project objectives, a written description of the project, the exact work that needs to be performed, and so on. Also in this section you may find information concerning Quality Assurance provisions, any required meeting schedules, inspection procedures, deficiency reports, qualification requirements for employees, procedures when engineering changes are necessary, and so on. For more information on Service contracts (especially more detail about their special requirements) see Chapter 6.

Section D:
Packaging and Marking

PACKAGING AND MARKING:

(a) Supplies shall be packed and marked in accordance with best commercial practice to prevent damage to property.

(b) The contractor shall enclose a PACKING LIST within each shipping container. The list shall include: (1) Order Number, (2) Line Item Number, (3) Brief Description, and (4) Quantity.

Commercial Packaging. The federal government uses the term "commercial packaging" to describe any packaging that is developed by the supplier. The American Society for Testing and Material develops and maintains commercial packaging standards that are widely followed and referenced throughout the commercial packaging arena. The Department of Defense has adopted the ASTM D 3951 (Standard Practice for Commercial Packaging) as its commercial standard. Other commercial standards may also apply, based on the product involved, and the agency's particular needs.

Agencies generally prefer to use commercial packaging and performance-based specifications whenever possible—that is, when it is cost-effective and will withstand anticipated conditions. Commercial packaging is now used extensively in some areas, such as medical supplies and subsistence. The Defense Logistics Agency has made extensive use of commercial packaging, in up to 90 percent of their transactions overall. The military services have also demonstrated expanded use of commercial packaging.

Military Packaging. The term "military packaging" is used to describe the standard packaging requirements developed by the Department of Defense, known as MIL-STD-2073-1. Traditional packaging methods, which would normally serve a commercial customer well, can be unsuitable for the more severe conditions that arise when that same product is shipped to a military customer. In these instances, more stringent military packaging requirements may be appropriate.

In this section of the solicitation package you will find the agency's packaging requirements. If possible the agency will specify a performance-based packaging requirement—that is, they will describe the required outcome and provide criteria for measuring and verifying performance, but they do not dictate the specific methods to be used to achieve those outcomes. In this case, you would propose an appropriate packaging plan, and work with the agency to agree on a mutually acceptable plan of action.

We discuss this in more detail in Chapter 7.

SECTION E:
INSPECTION AND ACCEPTANCE, AND
SECTION F:
DELIVERIES OR PERFORMANCE

```
SECTION E Inspection and Acceptance


INSPECTION AND ACCEPTANCE TERMS

Supplies/services will be inspected/accepted at:

CLIN      INSPECT AT          INSPECT BY      ACCEPT AT          ACCEPT BY
0001      Destination         Government      Destination        Government


SECTION F Deliveries or Performance


DELIVERY INFORMATION

CLINS     DELIVERY DATE       UNIT OF ISSUE QUANTITY FOB  SHIP TO ADDRESS
0001      22-SEP-03           Each          3.00    Dest. F44LGL
                                                          940 MXS/MXMG - F44LGL
                                                          MSGT. JACK LEWIS
                                                          8401 ARNOLD AVENUE, BLDG
                                                          1225
                                                          BEALE AFB CA 95903
```

Inspect/Accept. In this case the item will be inspected and accepted at the destination point. At other times the agency may wish to inspect the item at its point of manufacture.

Delivery Date. This is *not* the shipping date. Your product must *arrive* no later than this stated delivery date—*never* be late for this date!

FOB means Freight on Board—Destination. This means that you own the product until it reaches its destination.

Ship to Address. This section tells you where to ship the product. The alpha-numeric code at the beginning of the shipping address is used by the Department of Defense to identify each of their facilities where items are delivered, inspected, and accepted. You may come across the acronym DODAAC, or Department of Defense Activity Address Code.

SECTION G:
CONTRACT ADMINISTRATION DATA

This section discusses such things as payment via Electronic Funds Transfer and cites the appropriate section of the Federal Acquisition Regulation. Electronic invoicing via Wide Area Work Flow is discussed further in Chapter 7.

SECTION H:
SPECIAL CONTRACT REQUIREMENTS

Naturally our brief explanations are not meant as a substitute for a thorough reading of the regulations. That said, here is a sampling:

252.203-7002 Display of DOD Hotline Poster Dec/1991
252.204-7000 Disclosure of Information Dec/1991
252.205-7000 Provision of Information to Cooperative Agreement Holders Dec/1991
252.225-7002 Qualifying Country Sources As Subcontractors Apr/2003
252.225-7004 Reporting Of Contract Performance outside The United States Jun/2005

252.225-7005 Identification of Expenditures in the United States Jun/2005

252.225-7006 Quarterly Reporting Of Actual Contract Performance outside the U.S.

252.225-7013 Duty-Free Entry Jun/2005

252.225-7021 Trade Agreements Feb/2006

252.225-7033 Waiver of United Kingdom Levies Apr/2003

252.225-7043 Antiterrorism/Force Protection Policy for Defense Contractors outside the U.S.

252.226-7001 Utilization Of Indian Organizations, Indian-Owned Economic Sep/2004 Enterprises, and Native Hawaiian Small Business Concerns

252.228-7003 Capture and Detention Dec/1991

252.231-7000 Supplemental Cost Principles Dec/1991

252.246-7000 Material Inspection and Receiving Report Mar/2003

252.246-7001 Warranty of Data Dec/1991

252.237-7019 Training for Contractor Personnel Interacting With Detainees Aug/2005

252.217-7026 Identification of Sources of Supply

252.225-7040 Contractor Personnel Supporting a Force Deployed Outside the U.S.

52.204-4005 Required Use of Electronic Contracting

This is an example of a solicitation document in which the agency has made special note of certain Federal Acquisition Regulations that apply in this case. Any additional contract requirements will be listed in this section. Each solicitation document is different, and not all will have any regulations cited here.

Certain regulations may be cited more frequently, such as:

252.225-7004 (Reporting of Contract Performance outside the United States). If you will be sending employees overseas in order to complete the contract, then this section would be relevant, and you would need to carefully read this section to understand in detail the risks and responsibilities involved.

252.204-4005 (Required Use of Electronic Contracting) explains that in this case (and many other cases) contract awards, modifications, and delivery orders will be issued electronically, either via the Internet (WWW) or via Electronic Data Interchange (EDI). This regulation also explains in detail the requirements for EDI transactions via the Federal Acquisition Network (FACNET), including the EDI standards that are used, the requirement to complete EDI 838, the Trading Partner Profile, and information about the Value Added Network, or VAN you must select.

252.217-7026 (Identification of Sources of Supply). If this regulation is cited, the agency needs to obtain information concerning the sources of supply of any item it purchases. You must supply this information before the award, in a pre-determined table format that is explained in detail, listing the National Stock Number, Manufacturer address and part number, and so on.

Other special requirements might include a detailed explanation of how U.S. dollar to foreign currency rates are calculated, and so on.

SECTION I: CONTRACT CLAUSES

Section I refers to Contract Clauses that are relevant to this particular bid. Some are printed in full, whereas others are simply referenced, and it is your responsibility to read and understand them.

Many of these Contract Clauses concern standard business practices—to do with labor laws, equal opportunity regulations, and so on.

All the regulations can be found at the Federal Acquisition Regulations (FAR) Website: *www.arnet.gov/far.*

Here are some of the more common clauses you may come across.

Instructions to Offerors — Commercial Items (FAR 52.212-1)

52.212-1   INSTRUCTIONS TO OFFERORS – COMMERCIAL ITEMS (OCT 2000)

(a) North American Industry Classification System (NAICS) code and small business size standard. The NAICS code and small business size standard for this acquisition appear in Block 10 of the solicitation cover sheet (SF 1449). However, the small business size standard for a concern which submits an offer in its own name, but which proposes to furnish an item which it did not itself manufacture, is 500 employees.

(b) Submission of offers. Submit signed and dated offers to the office specified in this solicitation at or before the exact time specified in this solicitation. Offers may be submitted on the SF 1449, letterhead stationery, or as otherwise specified in the solicitation. As a minimum, offers must show—

(1) The solicitation number;

(2) The time specified in the solicitation for receipt of offers;

(3) The name, address, and telephone number of the offeror;

(4) A technical description of the items being offered in sufficient detail to evaluate compliance with the requirements in the solicitation. This may include product literature, or other documents, if necessary;

(5) Terms of any express warranty;

(6) Price and any discount terms;

(7) "Remit to" address, if different than mailing address;

This clause contains standard information that you must understand in order to be able to fulfill your obligations under this contract.

Offeror Representations and Certifications — Commercial Items (FAR 52.212-3)

A completed copy of this regulation must be submitted with every quote. A complete copy of this regulation has been provided for you at the end of this book. Once you have filled in the information required, keep the original and make copies to submit with all future quotes. In more and more cases agencies are requiring that this information be completed online via the Online Representation and Certification Website at *www.orca.bpn.gov*. This is discussed, in detail, in Chapter 1.

ACKNOWLEDGMENT OF SOLICITATION AMENDMENTS

Always check for any Amendments at the agency's Website where the original solicitation notice was posted, before you submit your offer. It is important to remember that any Amendments *must* be acknowledged by your signature and the date, and become part of your offer. Failure to include these Amendments with your offer will mean that your offer will not be eligible for consideration.

PAST PERFORMANCE INFORMATION

If you are requested to do so in the solicitation document, you must submit information about your recent past customers (Point of Contact name, company address, and telephone number) to the Open Ratings service, provided by the Dun & Bradstreet Company. Open Ratings will request information from these companies regarding your company's service: Did you deliver on time? Was the buyer satisfied with the overall product and the service they received? Did any problems get resolved quickly? This report will be sent to the appropriate government agency, so that they can be sure that they are dealing with a reputable company with a history of quality and service. You will be responsible for any costs incurred in creating this report, which is currently about $125.

The Open Ratings Website address is *www.openratings.com.*

CHANGES TO CONTRACT TERMS AND CONDITIONS

If you intend to add or delete any terms, conditions, and provisions included in the solicitation, you must specify these additions/deletions on a company letterhead attached to your offer.

FOR HOW LONG WILL THE PRICE YOU GIVE BE VALID?

You must honor the price that you have given for a certain number of days from the date for receipt of offers. The number of days for which you must guarantee your price may vary from one solicitation to another, so it is very important that you check this before you make your offer. In some cases, you must guarantee your prices for 30 days; in other cases it may be as long as 180 days!

SAMPLES

If the government requests a sample of your product, you must provide one.

LATE SUBMISSIONS, MODIFICATIONS, REVISIONS, AND WITHDRAWALS OF OFFERS

If your offer arrives late, the agency has the option whether or not to consider it. You may modify your offer, revise it, or withdraw it prior to a contract being awarded, even if it arrives after the bid opening date. Section F explains what a late offer is, and exactly how it will be handled. It is always a good idea to follow up to ensure that your offer arrived on time by contacting the Contracting Officer involved.

CONTRACT AWARD

In this section of a particular solicitation document you will notice that the agency is asking you to give them your best price, as this contract will be awarded without discussion. This particular contract is not a negotiated contract. Remember to always give the agency your *best* price!

MULTIPLE AWARDS

This means that more than one company can be awarded a contract under this solicitation number. At other times only one award will be made, and you will see the notation "all or none"

SPECIFICATIONS AND STANDARDS

This section tells you where to go to obtain additional documents such as specifications and standards that are cited in the solicitation. This section gives you agency addresses, phone numbers, fax numbers, and Websites so you can obtain any additional information pertaining to this quote.

EVALUATION—COMMERCIAL ITEMS (FAR 52.212-2)

52.212-2   EVALUATION – COMMERCIAL ITEMS (JAN 1999)

(a) The Government will award a contract resulting from this solicitation to the responsible offeror whose offer conforming to the solicitation will be most advantageous to the Government, price and other factors considered. The following factors shall be used to evaluate offers:

Technical and past performance, when compared to price is most important.

(b) Options. The Government will evaluate offers for award purposes by adding the total price for all options to the total price for the basic requirement. The Government may determine that an offer is unacceptable if the option prices are significantly unbalanced. Evaluation of options shall not obligate the Government to exercise the option(s).

(c) A written notice of award or acceptance of an offer, mailed or otherwise furnished to the successful offeror within the time for acceptance specified in the offer, shall result in a binding contract without further action by either party. Before the offer's specified expiration time, the Government may accept an offer (or part of an offer), whether or not there are negotiations after its receipt, unless a written notice of withdrawal is received before award.

(End of clause)

Evaluations. This provision lets you know exactly what criteria the government will use to evaluate your offer, and the method that will be used to award the contract.

In many cases, although price will be a factor, it will not necessarily be the only factor or even the determining factor in awarding the contract. Sometimes a company's past performance or technical ability will be more important. At other times, the delivery schedule will be a priority.

Options. In many cases, the agency will specify a certain quantity of an item, and then specify particular options that it may choose to exercise. For example, the agency may choose to exercise a 100-percent option, doubling the initial quantity requested.

Award. Once it has been accepted, the offer is binding.

CONTRACT TERMS AND CONDITIONS— COMMERCIAL ITEMS (FAR 52.212-4)

The information in this section explains the terms and conditions of this contract, so that you have a full understanding of what is required from the time you are awarded the contract until you are paid in full. Read through this section so that you fully understand your obligations to the government.

Note particularly the following sections:

Excusable delays. Make sure that you can honor the terms of the contract before you make an offer. Keep the Contracting Officer fully informed if you expect unavoidable delays in the completion of this contract.

Invoices. Pay particular attention to the format of the invoice you should submit to the government. You do not want any delays in the payment process because you omitted relevant information on your invoice!

In more and more cases the agencies are requiring businesses to use certain specific electronic invoicing software, such as Wide Area Work Flow. We discuss this further in Chapter 7.

Prices. Remember that when you consider the price you will quote to the agency, the terms of delivery must be taken into consideration, as well as any applicable taxes. The price you quote must be net—that is, it must include all applicable taxes and delivery costs. Unless stated otherwise, all unit prices submitted are for a delivered price.

Freight on Board (FOB) Destination means that you are paying the freight to the delivered address. You still own the product until the agency accepts it.

Freight on Board (FOB) Origin means that the agency owns the product once it leaves your premises.

CONTRACT TERMS AND CONDITIONS REQUIRED TO IMPLEMENT STATUTES OR EXECUTIVE ORDERS — COMMERCIAL ITEMS (FAR 52.212-5)

You will find these regulations in every solicitation document, but they do not all apply to every solicitation. The Contracting Officer will note which regulations pertain to a particular quote. Next to each regulation will be a box which the Contracting Officer will check if that particular regulation applies. (If the box is not checked, then that regulation does not apply.)

You should familiarize yourself with these regulations, so that you fully understand the terms of the contract. However, many of these regulations will not be relevant to a particular quote, and many regulations will appear each time you bid, so that you will soon become familiar with them.

More information concerning these regulations can be found on the Federal Acquisition Website: *http://farsite.hill.af.mil.*

MORE CITED REGULATIONS

Notice in this example that certain regulations (numbered here as 2 through 7) concern set-asides for small businesses or businesses in a HUB-Zone. These set-asides were described for you in Chapter 1.

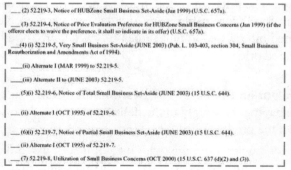

Labor Laws. Other sections of the regulations concern convict labor laws, child labor laws, equal-opportunity and affirmative-action laws, and so on. You are probably already aware of these regulations as they relate to your commercial business.

Environmental and Recycled Content (FAR 52.223-9). This regulation concerns environmentally friendly, recycled-content and other regulations that may be relevant to your company's products. A more detailed discussion of the federal government's Environmentally Friendly, or "Green" purchasing program is found in the chapter 3 which concerns the Defense Logistics Agency's DIBBS site.

Buy American and the Trade Agreements Acts (FAR 52.225). These regulations concern the Buy American Act, the North America Free Trade Agreement, and the restrictions that are placed on certain foreign purchases. If your product is made outside of the United States, Canada, or Mexico, you must be aware of the restrictions that the government places on purchases of foreign-made products. These regulations are contained in the Federal Acquisition Regulations FAR 52.225. You will find a list of "designated countries" in this section of the FAR. I have included a complete list of designated countries, and their corresponding 2-digit codes, in the Appendix section of this book.

Payments by Electronic Funds Transfers or Third Party Payments. You will be paid by Electronic Funds Transfer if this regulation is cited. The agency will use the information you provided when you registered at the Central Contractor Registration (CCR) site. It is very important that the payment information you provided when you registered at CCR is kept up-to-date, in order to avoid delays in getting paid.

Minimum Wage and Labor Laws. Certain regulations that are commonly found cited in this section refer to minimum wage laws and fair labor standards. You are probably already familiar with these laws as they apply to your commercial business. If you are a company that provides a service, you will find more information on minimum wages, and how these regulations may affect you, in Chapter 6, which discusses service contracts.

Access to Company Records. Certain federal regulations allow the agency access to your company's records, but only as they relate to this contract. You must be able to produce records relating to any government contract for three years after you have been paid.

Subcontracting Opportunities. In the case of larger contracts, regulations require that subcontracting opportunities for small businesses must be made available.

SECTION J:
LIST OF ATTACHMENTS

A list of any relevant drawings, meeting schedules, parts lists, and so on that are included as attachments will be in this section.

Exhibit A Contract Data Requirements List 10-July-2006

Attachment 001 ATPD 2277, Improved Bridge, Floating Ribbon, Interior Bay & Ramp Bay

Attachment 002 Graphic Representation of the IUID Plates

Attachment 003 Projected IRB Fielding Schedule for the IRB thru FY11

Attachment 004 Government Configuration Management Plan

Attachment 005 Listing of Parts under CLIN 1013AA

SECTION K:
REPRESENTATIONS, CERTIFICATIONS, AND OTHER STATEMENTS

This section contains the Representations & Certifications clauses that we discussed in Chapter 1, Important Business Codes and Numbers; specifically the section about registering at the new Online Representations and Certifications Application (ORCA) site.

You will need to renew your registration annually, or whenever your company information changes.

The **Place of Manufacture Clause** requires you to declare if your product is produced within or outside of the United States. This information is for statistical purposes only, and is not the same as the Buy American or Trade Agreement Act.

The Cost Accounting Standards Notices and Certification Clause is **FAR 52.230-1** and does not apply to small businesses, and it is only needed for contracts valued at greater than $500,000.

Clause **FAR 252.225-7020** concerns the Trade Agreements Certificate. The agency will only consider offers of end products that are made in the United States, or in another designated or qualifying country, unless the product is only available outside this list. In that case, you would list the item and its country of origin. A complete list of the current qualifying and designated countries is included in the Appendix.

FAR 252.247-7022 asks whether any of the items are going to be Transported by Sea.

FAR 52.215-4005 concerns the Minimum Acceptance Period (that is, the number of days that is available to the Government for awarding a contract, from the date that is specified in the solicitation for receipt of offers). The agency lists their minimum acceptance period, and asks that you add yours here.

FAR 52.215-4010 concerns your company's Authorized Negotiators—that is, you will list here the names of those people who are authorized to negotiate with the agency on your company's behalf, with regard to this contract.

FAR 52.223-4002 concerns the restricted use of Class I Ozone-Depleting Substances (CIODS), identified in Section 602(a) of the Clean Air Act, including chlorofluorocarbons (CFCs). The Department of Defense cannot award any contract that requires the use of CIODS, unless it is essential for contract performance, and no suitable substitute is available. You are asked to confirm the agency's finding on any items that contain CIODS that are essential to fulfill the contract, and to let the agency know if there are any known substitutes available.

SECTION L: INSTRUCTIONS, CONDITIONS, AND NOTICES

Federal Acquisition Regulations may be referenced either in full or in part in this section. Of course, we cannot include every regulation that may appear in this section, so you will need to carefully read each regulation that appears in the solicitation document. You will *also* need to check those regulations that are only referenced in the document, by searching at the FarSite Website to make sure that you understand how they apply to this offer.

Federal Acquisition Regulations can be found at:

www.arnet.gov/far/ and *http://farsite.hill.af.mil/.*

POSSIBLE CLAUSES

52.211-2 Availability of Specifications. Most unclassified Defense specifications and standards may be downloaded from the ASSIST Website (*http://assist.daps.dla.mil/*) or may be ordered from the Department of Defense Single Stock Point (DoDSSP). This regulation gives you exact details on how to obtain them.

52.211-14 Notice of Priority Rating for National Defense Use. This regulation discusses the Defense Priorities and Allocations System (DPAS). If this regulation is cited, then any contract awarded would be a DX Rated Order, and you would need to follow the instructions concerning this regulation. We discussed this regulation earlier in this chapter (Section A, Solicitation/Contract).

For more information on this program:

http://www.ml.afrl.afmil/dpas/dpas-what.html

http://guidebook.dcma.mil/38 DPAS%20Guidebook.htm.

52.214-34 and 52.214-35 Submission of Offers in the English Language and in U.S. Currency. You must submit your offers in the English language, and in U.S. dollars.

52.215-1 Instructions to Offerors—Competitive Acquisitions. This regulation discusses in detail how to submit, revise, or withdraw your proposal.

52.216-1 Type of Contract. If the contract is a Firm-Fixed Price (FFP) contract then there can be no adjustments to the price during the life of the contract. At other times, contracts may be Fixed Price with Economic Price Adjustments; Fixed Ceiling Price Contracts; Level of Effort Contracts, Cost Reimbursement Contracts; Cost-Sharing Contracts; Contracts with Incentives; Time & Materials Contracts; Labor Hour Contracts; and so on.

52.233-2 Service of Protest. Policies and procedures for filing a protest.

52.211-4047 Notice to Offerors Intending To Offer Other Than New Material. This section discusses whether you may offer a remanufactured or reconditioned product, or whether the item must be new.

52.245-4002 Acquisition of New Facilities, Special Test Equipment, or Special Tooling. The agency will not reimburse you for the cost of any new facilities, special test equipment, or special tooling as a separate item. However, you may choose to amortize any of these costs in your submitted price.

52.245-4003 Use of Existing Government-Owned Property. At times the agency may furnish you with an item in order for you to fulfill your contract. For example, if a service contract involves the repair or upgrade of a particular piece of government-owned equipment. At other times, you may request the use of government-owned facilities, tools, or other special test equipment. In that case, you would need to include the written permission of the Contracting Officer when you submit your offer.

Section M:
Evaluation Factors

The agency will evaluate all the offers it receives, and base their award decision on what they determine to be in the best interests of the Government. Your proposal will be evaluated in three areas:

1. Price.
2. Past Performance.
3. Technical/Management.

In some cases, price alone is the determining factor, and at other times the agency may give equal weight to various other factors.

In this section of the solicitation document, the agency will clearly state how they will make their evaluation and how price, technical ability, Past Performance, or other factors will be weighed when making their decision.

In cases where technical requirements are critical, the agency may convene a Technical/Management Evaluation Panel, which will analyze each Technical/Management Proposal that is submitted, and will then rate each element, giving the highest rating to the best overall approach. Naturally, in these cases, the Technical/ Management and Past Performance factors become significantly more important than Price.

In some instances, the agency will assign a rating to each factor, depicting how well you meet the requirements in each area. For example, your evaluation will be rated highest if your proposal meets or exceeds the requirements of the solicitation, if you show a very good solution for meeting the needs and objectives of the program, if you have significant strengths in certain critical areas, and so on.

The Past Performance evaluation tries to determine whether your company will successfully complete the requirements of the contract, based on your previous performance in both current and past contracts. The agency will look at past contracts that are relevant to the current requirement, and are as up-to-date as possible. The agency will look at previous contracts with federal, state, or local governments, as well as commercial contracts when making their evaluation. If there were any problems with the contract, the agency will take into consideration whether they were appropriately and effectively addressed—not just whether promises were kept, or plans were fulfilled!

If you have no record of Past Performance, or if Past Performance information is not available, then the agency will give you a "neutral" rating in this area. That is, you will not be evaluated favorably or unfavorably on Past Performance.

The Past Performance Information Retrieval System is the site where government agencies note how well you performed on any awarded contract, and this information is shared among other government agencies. You can have access to your own records, and may comment upon anything in the report, but you do *not* have access to the records of other contractors.

https://www.ppirs.gov/

COMBINED SYNOPSIS/SOLICITATION

Some small bids are combined synopsis/solicitations. In these instances, there is no Solicitation packet. The combined Synopsis/Solicitation will not contain any administrative paperwork, but will reference all the rules and regulations pertaining to this proposal. The regulations are referenced by a Federal Acquisition Regulation (FAR) number, followed by a subject name (for example: FAR 52.212-3 Offeror Representation and Certifications). It will be your responsibility to check at the FAR Website (*http://farsite.hill.af.mil*), and to find the details for each regulation that has been referenced.

Because there is no solicitation standard form in these cases, you will be required to submit your offer on your company's letterhead. You will also need to include FAR regulation 52.212-3, entitled Offeror Representations and Certifications. If this portion of your offer is not submitted, your offer may not be considered. A complete copy of this regulation is included in the Appendix, so that you can either fill this out once and submit a copy each time you submit an offer, or complete this section online via the ORCA Website. (See Chapter 1 for a discussion of this requirement.)

SUBMITTING YOUR OFFER

Once your quote is completed and signed, if you are required to mail it, be sure to include:

- The original solicitation document *plus* the number of required copies.
- Any Amendments, which must also be signed and dated.

- Any other additional information, such as catalogues, sales sheets, price lists, and so on.
- In the bottom left-hand corner of the envelope, write the Solicitation number, and the Bid Opening Date and Time. This will allow your bid to be sent to the correct department as quickly as possible, and will avoid any delays.

Last, but certainly not least:

Be sure your quote arrives on time!

CHAPTER 6

SERVICE CONTRACTS

Are you a landscaping company, a public relations firm, a temporary staffing agency, a construction firm, a computer programming company, a janitorial/facilities management agency, or any other type of service-oriented company?

If so, this chapter is for you!

Although much of the information in the previous chapters applies to both product and service contracts, there are some special requirements that you will need to be aware of if your company provides a service.

Of course, there is an enormous difference between different types of service companies. A landscaping company looking to be awarded a contract for grounds maintenance at a particular agency site will need to cover a specific set of criteria, but a public relations firm will need another very different approach. There are still some general rules that apply in any service contract, regardless of type.

In many cases the solicitation document for a service contract will require that you submit your proposal in three distinct parts:

1. The Price Proposal.
2. The Technical Proposal.
3. Past Performance Information.

The solicitation document will state clearly how to complete each one of these parts and you will need to pay a great deal of attention to the details in these sections. In many cases, the failure to follow exactly the requirements that are set out here can result in your proposal not even being given consideration. All that hard work for naught, because you didn't submit exactly what was asked!

Part One—The Price Proposal

This section is fairly straightforward, and a lot of the information required is the same as that discussed earlier—completing the cover sheet or SF1449 that includes your company information, Dun & Bradstreet (DUNS) number, your Commercial and Government Entity (CAGE) codes, and so on. You would also include the Representations & Certifications document (ORCA), and pricing for the service to be performed.

Part Two—The Technical Proposal

This section is probably the one that will take most of your time to prepare. Remember, however, that it is likely that you will be able to use this information again in future submissions, with only minor changes each time to reflect the requirements of a particular contract document.

In many instances the agency will set a limit of the number of pages you may submit in this section, and they will often require you to submit these documents in a particular format and font style, using double- or single-spaced type and so on. Pay particular attention to this. You don't want your carefully prepared proposal to be rejected because of a minor error such as using the wrong fontor size. Also, because the agency will often limit the number of pages you can submit here, you want to make the best use of each page, and make sure you cover each requirement thoroughly.

Read through the requirements of the Technical Proposal carefully before you begin to gather information. You may be able to find a lot of the information you need in your existing marketing literature-company brochures, Websites, and so on—which can then be tailored to the specifics of the requirements. In many cases, this section will reflect the way you submit offers in the commercial environment.

The first thing here is to read through the Statement of Work (SOW), the Performance Work Statement (PWS), or the Statement of Objectives (SOO) section carefully. Often, the agency will describe what they need line-by-line, so be sure your proposal fully covers each requirement that is listed

If the project requires it, you may be asked to describe your overall project management plan, the functions of each team member on the project, and the procedures you will put in place to ensure that deliverables are met, including cost control measures, project schedules, and staffing requirements. If you are planning a teaming or subcontracting approach to this project, you should show how you will maintain a unified effort, and how the team will interact with the agency.

In many cases the requirements of the Statement of Work will be broken down into smaller tasks, and a specific timetable for delivery of each task will be laid out, as we can see in this example:

SOW Paragraph Reference	Deliverable Description	Delivery Date NLT (no later than):
General	Deliverables—All deliverables become the property of the United States government. Unless otherwise stated, all deliverables will be submitted in both hardcopy and electronic media in Microsoft Word/PowerPoint/Excel format.	

1.0	Completed analysis or assessment—Completed draft analysis or assessment in the appropriate Joint Staff Study format. Presented in briefing, written report, and/or white paper format.	NLT 5 days prior to suspense
3.0	Briefing describing strategies and analysis campaign plans—Summarize current analysis strategies and campaign plans for the major department processes.	NLT 10 days after Government tasking
4.0	Briefing summarizing results of literature searches—Briefing identifying the general issue area to be researched.	NLT 10 days after Government tasking
5.0	Research and decisional meeting briefings—Draft briefing to scope requirements.	NLT 10 days after Government tasking
6.1	Analytic Tools Briefing—Draft briefing and point papers assessing new analytic tools/methodologies/emerging technologies.	20 days following technology ID
6.2	CCB Briefs and Tool Management Reports—Draft briefing and information package for Configuration Control Board meetings; draft CM plans and process reports.	5 pays prior to board
7.1	Scoping research briefings—Draft briefings and papers summarizing research to scope analytical requirements, tools, and methodologies.	NLT 20 Workdays following tasking
7.2	M&S Topic Report—Draft written response to *milestone and schedule* issues in standard Joint Staff format.	10 workdays following task ID

8.1	Status Tracking Report—Monitor, track and compile database spreadsheet representations of the status of studies based on their timelines, milestones and progress reports.	10 workdays prior to end of each month
8.2	Reports, summaries and briefings—Prepare draft reports, study summaries, formal briefings, and supporting graphic material in written or oral form All documentation shall be provided in hard copy and electronic format and shall be rendered in the current Joint Staff version of Microsoft Office applications.	NLT 5 days prior to suspense
8.4	Meeting support—Provide support by organizing technical interchanges and support discussions, preparing meeting minutes and after-action reports, coordinating and integrating study results with other organizations, and distributing materials. This includes offsite government-sponsored conferences and seminars.	NLT 5 days after event
8.5	Scheduling support—The contractor shall provide support scheduling issues for the FM FCB. This includes monitoring JCIDS documents and milestones in order to develop and provide recommendation summaries and status reports to the government.	3 workdays following task ID
9.0	Quality Control Plan—	10 days after contract award
1.0,2.0,3.0, 4.0,5.0	Monthly Status Reports—	By the 5th workday each month

Part Three — Past Performance Information

The agency is looking for clear evidence that you have performed work of a similar nature in the past, and that your previous work was satisfactory. To this end you will be asked to supply information on previous customers, so that the agency can contact them and evaluate your performance. You may be asked for any customer surveys demonstrating customer satisfaction with overall performance, and the quality of completed job, and how well problems or delays were resolved, if any occurred. You also may be asked for details of any federal contracts you have previously completed, as well as any recent commercial projects.

If you plan a teaming or subcontracting arrangement with another company you will need to provide complete information on how this will work, and if you have teamed with this contractor on previous occasions.

Wage Determinations

Federal Acquisition Regulation Part 22 describes how existing labor laws apply to government contracts. Federal agencies must encourage contractors to cooperate with federal and state labor requirements such as safety, health and sanitation, maximum hours and minimum wages, equal employment opportunity, child and convict labor, age discrimination, disabled and Vietnam veteran employment, and employment of the handicapped.

Wage determinations are available at the Department of Labor's Website: *www.wdol.gov*.

At this site, federal contracting officers can find the appropriate wage determinations for their particular contract. You can also research the prevailing wage determinations for your company's area of expertise here.

For example:

- The Davis-Bacon Act covers federal construction projects.

- The McNamara-O'Hara Service Contract Act covers service employees.

- The Contract Work Hours and Safety Standards Act requires you to pay time-and-a-half for all hours worked more than 40 hours, and also prohibits unsanitary, hazardous, or dangerous working conditions.

- The Copeland "Anti-Kickback" Act prohibits you from inducing an employee to give up any compensation to which he or she is entitled. This act also requires you to submit a weekly statement of the wages paid to each employee.

- The Walsh-Healey Public Contracts Act requires you to pay minimum-wage rates and overtime pay on federal contracts to manufacture or furnish materials, supplies, or equipment.

CONTRACTOR MANPOWER REPORTING

If your contract is with the Army, you will be required to report annually on all manpower required to perform this contract. The Contractor Manpower Reporting Application (CMRA) Website is *https://cmra.army.mil.*

You will need to provide details on the contracting office, the contract number, the date of the reporting period, your company information (name, address, telephone, and so forth), the estimated number of labor hours and the estimated dollar amount paid, the Federal Service Code that applies to this contract, your estimated data collection costs, the location where the contract is performed, and the number of employees involved.

When you submit an offer you may choose to charge the government a fee for compliance with this requirement, or alternatively you may choose to waive this fee in your proposal.

Insurance (FAR 52.228-5)

You are responsible for making sure that you have the required insurance for this contract. Please refer to Part 28 of the Federal Acquisition Regulations, which can be found at the FAR Website: *http://farsite.hill.af.mil.* This section covers Bonds and Insurance, including such things as Workers Compensation and Liability Insurance requirements. This regulation does not always apply to all service contracts.

Site Visit (FAR 52.237-1)

In many cases it will be either suggested or required that you perform a site visit, so that you can see the conditions that may affect the cost of the contract. If you choose not to inspect the site before you submit your offer, then this cannot be grounds for a claim after the contract has been awarded.

Federal Travel Regulations

The Code of Federal Regulations (CFR) 41, Chapters 300 through 304, contain the policies that concern travel by federal civilian employees and others authorized to travel at government expense (Federal Travel Regulation, or FTR). If travel is a necessary part of any contract, the solicitation will describe exactly what is covered.

For more information on the Federal Travel Regulation (FTR) go to the General Services Administration Website at *www.gsa.gov/ft* or the Department of Defense Travel Regulations & the Joint Travel Regulations (JTR) at *https://secureapp2.hqda.pentagon.mil/perdiem/trvlregs.html.*

EVALUATING YOUR OFFER

FAR 52.212-2 describes how the agency will evaluate the offers it receives. The award will be made to the best overall (best value) proposal—that is, the offer that the agency considers to be the most beneficial to the government.

The agency will look at four evaluation factors:

1. Technical Approach.
2. Management Approach.
3. Past Performance.
4. Price.

Remember: The award may not necessarily be made to the lowest-priced offer.

In the solicitation document, the agency will list these evaluation factors in their order of importance. In some cases, the Technical Approach will be significantly more important; at other times Management, Price, or Past Performance may take precedence.

Technical Approach: The agency is looking for clear evidence that you fully understand the technical requirements that are necessary to complete the tasks or objectives laid out in solicitation's Statement of Work (SOW) or Performance Work Statement (PWS). Your proposal will need to show that you have the skills, knowledge, and capabilities to successfully perform all the required tasks, including in-depth knowledge of the field in question, an understanding of the regulations and codes that may apply to this particular contract, familiarity with the applications commonly used in this field, and so on.

Management Approach: The agency will be looking for evidence that you can provide personnel who are qualified in the field, and that your management plan will ensure that the contract is completed on time and budget. Does your management plan allow you to properly oversee your personnel and ensure quality deliverables? You must be able to demonstrate sound business practices, stable fiscal control, and so on.

Past Performance: The agency will look at how well you performed on recent similar contracts, either in the federal or commercial areas. You should include all your relevant past contracts, and show how you handled any problems as they arose. If you have no available past performance information, this section of the evaluation will be regarded as "neutral,"—that is, neither favorably nor unfavorably.

Price: In many service proposals, your proposed price will be less important than your technical and management approaches and your past performance. Your proposal must demonstrate reasonable pricing that is aligned with the technical and management approaches.

The agency will assign an **adjectival rating** to the technical and management approaches of your submission.

Rating	Definition
Outstanding	A proposal that satisfies all of the government's requirements with extensive detail to indicate feasibility of the approach and shows a thorough understanding of the problems and offers numerous significant strengths, which are not offset by weaknesses, with an overall low degree of risk in meeting the government's requirements.
Good	A proposal that satisfies all of the government's requirements with adequate detail to indicate feasibility of the approach and shows an understanding of the problems and offers some significant strengths or numerous minor strengths, which are not offset by weaknesses, with an overall low to moderate degree of risk in meeting the government's requirements.

Acceptable	A proposal that satisfies all of the government's requirements with minimal detail to indicate feasibility of the approach and shows a minimal understanding of the problems, with an overall moderate to high degree of risk in meeting the government's requirements.
Marginal	A proposal that satisfies all of the government's requirements with minimum detail to indicate feasibility of approach and shows a minimal understanding of the problem with an overall high degree of risk in meeting the government's requirement.
Unacceptable	A proposal that contains a major error(s), omission(s), or deficiency(ies) that indicates a lack of understanding of the problems or an approach that cannot be expected to meet requirements or involves a very high risk; and none of these conditions can be corrected without a major rewrite or revision of the proposal.

The agency may also assign an adjectival rating to the Past Performance section of your submission.

Rating	Description
Low Risk	Little doubt exists, based on the Offeror's performance record, that the Offeror can perform the proposed effort.
Moderate Risk	Some doubt exists, based on the Offeror's performance record, that the Offeror can perform the proposed effort.
High Risk	Significant doubt exists, based on the Offeror's performance record, that the Offeror can perform the proposed effort.
Unknown Risk	Little or no relevant offeror performance record identifiable; equates to a neutral rating having no positive or negative evaluation significance.

A-76 STANDARD
STREAMLINED COMPETITIONS

In 1998, the Office of Management and Budget's Circular No. A-76 established a Competitive Sourcing Program, which aims to increase efficiency and reduce government costs. The A-76 guidelines encourages competition and tries to provide a level playing field between public and private offers. In an A-76 competition, the agency will look for proposals that meet their current needs from both private industry and from the government organization that is currently performing the work.

Examples of these types of competitions could include services such as computer facilities management services, data entry services, database management and IT services, office administrative services (mail clerk or file clerk, for example), various support services, and facility management, and operations services.

The Federal Activities Inventory Reform (FAIR) Act requires agencies to make an annual inventory of the commercial activities that are currently performed by federal employees and submit them to the Office of Management and Budget.

There are two different types of A-76 competition:

1. In a **Standard Competition**, an agency issues a solicitation and selects a service provider based on the offers it receives. At the same time the agency also develops a "most efficient organization" that will form the basis for the agency's offer in the competition. This typically involves streamlining the existing organization, and aims to place the government in the best competitive position against the private sector offers. A Standard Competition is usually completed within 12 months of a public announcement.

2. In a **Streamlined Competition**, an agency determines an estimated contract price for performing the work by an outside contractor. The agency

will do this either by soliciting proposals from prospective contractors or by conducting its own market research. For example, by looking at current multiple award schedule contracts. The agency then determines how much it costs to perform the function in-house, either using the organization as it currently exists, or as it will be configured after proposed streamlining has taken effect.

After the costs for both the public and private sectors are compared, the best value organization wins. A Streamlined Competition is usually completed within 90 days from public announcement.

In order to determine the in-house cost of a particular function the agency must follow certain regulations or guidelines that are listed in Attachment C of OMB Circular A-76. The agency may also use a software program called COMPARE (*www.comparea76.com*).

MORE RESOURCES

The Acquisition Center for Excellence Services (ACES) Website provides best practices information: *https:// acc.dau.mil/ace.*

CHAPTER 7

FULFILLING THE TERMS OF YOUR CONTRACT

PACKING AND MARKING REQUIREMENTS

Commercial Packaging: The federal government uses the term "commercial packaging" to describe any packaging that is developed by the supplier. The American Society for Testing and Material (ASTM) develops and maintains commercial packaging standards that are widely followed and referenced throughout the commercial packaging arena. The Department of Defense has adopted the ASTM D 3951, "Standard Practice for Commercial Packaging," as its commercial standard. Other commercial standards may also apply, based on the product involved, and the agency's particular needs.

Agencies generally prefer to use commercial packaging and performance-based specifications whenever possible—that is, when it is cost-effective and will withstand anticipated conditions.

Military Packaging: The term "military packaging" is used to describe the standard packaging requirements developed by the Department of Defense, known as MIL-STD-2073-1. Traditional packaging methods, which would normally serve a commercial customer well, can be unsuitable for the more severe conditions that arise when that same product is shipped to a military customer. In these instances more stringent military packaging requirements may be appropriate.

The agency may specify a performance-based packaging requirement—that is, they will describe the required outcome and provide criteria for measuring and verifying performance, but they do not dictate the specific methods to be used to achieve those outcomes. In this case, you would propose an appropriate packaging plan, and work with the agency involved to agree on a mutually-acceptable plan of action.

LIABILITY FOR DAMAGE CAUSED BY INADEQUATE PACKAGING

If the contract has specified Commercial Packing then you will assume liability for items packaged in accordance with normal commercial practices, if the damage is the result of faulty packaging.

However, the government accepts full responsibility for items packaged in accordance with military specifications. It is your responsibility to exactly follow the requirements of the military specifications listed in the contract, but the agency will be responsible for any losses incurred if the packaging does not provide adequate protection. Naturally, you are still liable for other defects or deficiencies in the delivered item—that is, defects that are *not* caused by inadequate military packaging or handling.

UNIQUE IDENTIFICATION OF ITEMS — BAR CODES AND RFID TAGS

The Department of Defense must establish accountability records for all items with a unit acquisition cost of $5,000 or greater, as well as for *all* sensitive or classified items, or items furnished to third parties. The Unique Identification of Items (UII) uses machine-readable data (bar codes, RFID tags, and so on) to allow the Department of Defense to distinguish one item from all other like and unlike items.

More information on this requirement can be found at *www.acq.osd.mil/dpap/UID*.

BAR CODES

For the Defense Supply Centers, bar code markings are required on all containers and loose or unpacked items. At one time, the military standard for bar codes was known as LOGMARS, but this no longer applies. Now, the military has adopted the commercial bar code standard ISO/IEC 16388 for all their bar code requirements.

You will need to apply a bar code containing the National Stock Number (NSN) on all unit packs and intermediate containers. Any exterior container should be bar coded with both the NSN and the contract number. This is required even for small items, which would need to have the bar code on an attached tag.

If you are *not* shipping the item to a DLA Distribution Depot (known as DVD, or Direct Vendor Delivery), you will also need to include other relevant information such as the document number, Routing Identifier Code, Unit of Issue, quantity, condition code, distribution code, and unit price information. This information should be put onto labels that are then attached to DD Form 250, the Material Inspection and Receiving Report.

For more details on bar code requirements, go to the DSCC's site (*www.dscc.dla.mil/offices/packaging*).

RADIO FREQUENCY IDENTIFICATION (RFID) TAGS

The Department of Defense (DOD) requires that you use passive Radio Frequency Identification (RFID) tags, at the case and palletized unit load levels, when shipping certain items to certain DOD locations. The agency has plans to extend this requirement, to include shipments to *any* Department of Defense location for all items that require a Unique Identifier (UID).

By using your Commercial and Government Entity (CAGE) code information, you will be able to generate serial numbers that are unique to your shipping facility.

You will be required to provide information about the shipment in advance, via the Wide Area Work Flow system (WAWF). WAWF uses EDI Transaction Set # 856 for Advance Shipment Notices, where you will provide information including the contract number, the shipment date, the National Stock Number (NSN), the item description, the quantity, and the RFID tag number.

If your company does not already use RFID tagging, don't despair! You may choose to use a third-party provider to complete this work, or you may purchase pre-programmed Department of Defense compliant tags. Alternatively, if you are expecting to make multiple shipments to the Department of Defense, then you may choose to purchase a printer with blank tags, which will allow you to program and print them in-house.

For more information visit the DOD Website at *www.dodrfid.org*.

Your local Procurement Technical Assistance Center (PTAC) will also offer free training and assistance.

WOOD PACKAGING MATERIAL

Wood packaging material means wooden pallets or skids, as well as wooden boxes or crates. It does not include fiberboard, plywood, particleboard, or veneers. Since 2006 the Department of Defense has required that any wood packaging material used in shipping must meet certain international standards that are designed to block the movement of pests from one nation to another. If you are going to use any wood packaging material to ship items to the Department of Defense you must meet these standards.

For more information please go to the Dept. of Defense Packaging Information site at *www.dscc.dla.mil/Offices/Packaging/NMWPMnotice.htm*.

MORE INFORMATION

Mil-Std 2073 1D contains the standards for military packaging.

Mil-Std 129P provides information on standards military marking requirements.

Federal Standards 313 D (FED-STD-313D) contains information on Material Safety Data Sheets and Hazardous materials.

The Defense Logistics Agency (DLA) Website has more detailed information on Packaging, Specifications, Standards: *www.dscc.dla.mil/Offices/Packaging/specstdslist.html*

Packaging and Marking Requirements can also be found at the Acquisition Streamlining and Standardization Information System (ASSIST) Website:*http://assist.daps.dla.mil.*

The Department of Defense Materiel Management Regulation is DOD 4140.1-R.

The Department of Defense Standard Practice for Military Marking is MIL-STD-129.

The Department of Defense Standard Practice for Military Packaging is MIL-STD-2073-1.

The American Society for Testing and Material (ASTM) Standard Practice for Commercial Packaging IS ASTM D 3951.

SHIPPING YOUR PRODUCT

DD250: THE DISTRIBUTION DATA REPORT

You must provide the proper shipping documentation when you ship your products. You must complete the Distribution Data Report (DD250) before your first shipment for each deliverable item. This information is used by the government for estimating shipment costs, storage planning, and transport security. You will be told where the report should be e-mailed, and if any other copies of this report are required.

The form requests such information as the item size and weight, a description of the unit packaging, the shipping container, and the unitized load. You will also need to indicate any special requirements, for example any licenses or security needed for transporting the item, whether the item is considered to be dangerous goods for transport, or if the item requires electrostatic or magnetic sensitive marking. In certain instances, you should also indicate if the shelf life of the item is less than one year from the date of manufacture. For example, for food items, medicines, batteries, paints, sealants, adhesives, photographic film, tires, chemicals, packaged petroleum products, hoses/belts, o-rings, or for biological or chemical equipment and clothing.

Form DD 250, a commercial packing list, or the Wide Area Work Flow Receiving Report must be attached to the outside of the shipping container.

INSPECTION AND ACCEPTANCE

INSPECTION

When the product reaches its destination, it is inspected to ensure that it complies with the contract requirements. There are several levels of inspection depending on the contract involved.

When the contract does not exceed the simplified acquisition threshold of $100,000, the agency will generally rely on you for overall inspection, unless the contracting officer decides that some form of government inspection and testing is necessary. (FAR 52.246-1)

Federal Acquisition Regulation (FAR) 52.212-4 includes information about the inspection and acceptance of commercial items. You must ensure that the items or services you supply conform to the requirements of the contract. The government reserves the right to inspect or test any items.

FAR 52.246-2 is the Standard Inspection Requirement. In this case, the agency requires that you set up an inspection system that is acceptable to them.

The Higher-Level Contract Quality Requirement clause (FAR 52.246-11) is used when the contract has more stringent technical requirements. If this clause is cited in the contract, you must agree to comply with more stringent government inspection or quality assurance procedures. An example of this type of higher-level quality control standard would be ISO 9000. (FAR 46.202-4)

ACCEPTANCE

Once they have been inspected, the agency will officially accept the product or approve a specific service rendered. If the item or service does not conform to the requirements, you must correct the deficiency by a specified date. Supplies or services that do not conform to the contract requirements are classified in one of three ways:

1. Critical Non-Conformance is likely to result in hazardous or unsafe conditions for those who use or depend on the supplies or services.

2. Major Non-Conformance will result in the failure of the supplies or services or make it unusable for its intended purpose.

3. Minor Non-Conformance will not render the supplies unusable and the defect has little bearing on its effective use or operation.

No matter how slight a defect, strictly the government is entitled to reject an item if it does not conform to all the specifications in the contract. Normally, however, the government will only reject a product if the defect affects safety, health, reliability, durability, performance, or any other basic objective.

The Material Inspection and Receiving Report is known as DD 250.

Mil-Std 1916 is the Military Standard for Acceptance of Products.

INVOICING

WEB INVOICING SYSTEM (WINS)

WINS is a free service of the Defense Finance and Accounting Service (DFAS) that allows you to invoice the Department of Defense quickly, cheaply, and accurately, which can dramatically speed up the time it takes for you to receive payment.

Web Invoicing allows you to submit invoices and vouchers electronically. You can enter your invoices into the system, and the system checks to make sure that the information you submit is correct the first time. This significantly cuts down much of the paperwork involved, and gets your invoice into the DFAS system usually within 24 hours. Web Invoicing is free to vendors doing business with the government.

The system can be used from any Windows computer that has Internet access. There is no need to save any files on the computer, and you don't need to supply any personal certificates in order to log in. Dial-up access and AOL are also acceptable.

You can control the login for your WINS account and share it with as many or as few employees as you like. If you have more than one facility, and therefore more than one Commercial and Government Entity (CAGE) code, you can see and perform billing for all of them without having to log in and out for each one.

Web Invoicing System (WINS): *https://ecweb.dfas.mil*

Defense Finance and Accounting Service, Vendor/Contract Payments: *www.dod.mil/dfas/contractorpay.html*

WIDE AREA WORKFLOW

WHAT IS WIDE AREA WORKFLOW (WAWF)?

In October 2006, the Department of Defense made use of this system mandatory for all its vendors, and other government agencies are quickly following suit.

Wide Area Work Flow (WAWF) is a Web-based invoicing and reporting system that allows both you and the agency to track an item through its contract lifecycle. Using this system you will be able to quickly check the status of your contract and payments.

For each step of the way (shipping, receiving, acceptance, invoicing, to payment), you and the agency will be able to check the status of your documents. If a document is rejected for any reason, it will be easy for you to correct it and re-submit it electronically. This means a faster turnaround time and quicker payment of your invoice. You will be able to submit invoices and receiving reports electronically, track the status of any document, receive updates via e-mail whenever the status changes, and re-submit rejected documents.

GETTING STARTED

First check that you are registered at the Central Contractors Registration site (see Chapter 1). Then, decide on who, in the company, will be the Electronic Business Point of Contact (EB POC) and the Alternate Point of Contact (AEB POC). These people will determine which of your employees will be authorized to have access to the system and will be able to track, submit, and modify data on your behalf. You will also need an e-mail account for sending and receiving the documents, as you will be notified via e-mail whenever there are any changes. Each person who will be using the system will need to register at the site, and they will gain access to the system using either a User ID and password, or via a Public Key Infrastructure (PKI) certificate, if you prefer. If you wish, you may allow certain employees to have "view-only" access to documents.

SUBMITTING INVOICES

You will be able to submit Invoices and Receiving Reports electronically using an Interactive Web Application, Electronic Data Interchange (EDI), or Secure File Transfer Protocol (SFTP).

EDI and SFTP are suitable if you will be submitting many invoices or reports. The interactive Web application is suitable if you do *not* have a lot of invoices or reports to submit at any one time. Most vendors use the manual, Web-entry method to input their documents directly into WAWF. This is a good method if you have a small volume of payment documents to create, or if you have a small number of lines on your contract.

You will also need to register for Electronic Document Access, to be able to view details of contracts your company has been awarded. The Website is *http://eda.ogden.disa.mil.*

Once you have submitted your Invoice or Receiving Report, your designated Point of Contact will receive e-mails whenever any action is taken by the agency. For example, if a Receiving Report or an invoice is rejected for any reason, you will be able to quickly correct the data and resubmit. You will also be able to view previously submitted documents and check on their status.

WIDE AREA WORKFLOW TRAINING

Free Web-based training is available at *www.wawftraining.com.*

Also at this site, if you click on the "Resources" button in the top right corner, you can find many links to other information sites specifically for vendors using this system.

USING WIDE AREA WORKFLOW FOR VENDORS— A STUDENT GUIDE

This is quite a large file to download, at more than 250 pages, but it is full of useful information about the system.

http://www.dod.mil/dfas/contractorpay/electroniccommerce/ ECToolBox/WAWFVendorGuide3.pdf

PRACTICE SITES

You can practice using the system at these training sites, before you submit your first "live" invoice:

- *https://wawftraining.eb.mil.*
- *www.X12.org* Electronic Data Interchange (EDI) formats.
- *www.dfas.mil/ecedi* (EDI) implementation guides.

THE POST-AWARD ORIENTATION CONFERENCE

After the contract has been awarded, the agency will contact you at your place of business, usually through a phone call or a letter. This is known as a Post-Award Orientation Conference.

The Administrative Contracting Officer (ACO) will work with you to answer any questions you may have concerning the fulfillment of your contract. (Remember, however, that this is *not* a substitute for taking the time to understand the contract requirements before you make your offer, and it cannot change any terms of the contract once it has been awarded.)

The Administrative Contracting Officer will discuss with you any technical aspects of the contract, how to prevent any problems before they arise, and agree with you on common issues. He or she will identify and review specific key requirements and milestones that were identified in the contract. This conference could be particularly useful to you if this is your first government contract.

Often the aim of these conferences is simply to establish a good working relationship with you and give you a specific Point of Contact for any issues you may wish to discuss.

CONTRACT PERFORMANCE MONITORING

The agency will monitor your performance in any contract that you are awarded. Do you deliver the supplies or services on time? Are the items of a satisfactory quality? Did you fulfill all the terms laid out in the contract?

Contracts for commercial items will usually rely on your existing quality assurance system, rather than on an agency's inspection and testing. However, remember that even in commercial contracts the government *never* waives its rights to conduct its own inspection.

REPORTING

Progress Reports may be required to ensure that you remain on schedule, and to check on any possible delays. Sometimes the contract requires a Production Progress Report. These reports must be submitted by you on time. The Contracting Officer is authorized to withhold payments of up to 5 percent of the total contract amount or up to a maximum of $25,000, if these reports are delayed.

BREACH OF CONTRACT

A breach of contract is a failure, without legal excuse, to perform any promise that forms the whole or part of a contract. The agency can be guilty of a breach of contract if it issues a change that is outside the scope of the contract, or if it fails to disclose certain necessary information. You can be guilty of a breach of contract if you fail to perform the terms of the contract, or if you act fraudulently.

If the agency feels there may be a breach of contract, they will notify you of the problem and give you an opportunity to correct it. Certain delays may be excusable under the contract terms (for example, if they are caused by acts of god, fire, flood, extreme weather, and so on). If necessary, the Contracting Officer will issue a Stop-Work Order until the issues are resolved.

PERFORMANCE REPORTS

Federal agencies keep reports on how well you fulfill the terms of your contract, and share this information with other agencies to support future award decisions. They will be looking at the quality of the product or service you provide, whether you delivered on schedule, cost control, business relations, customer satisfaction, and so on.

Ratings can range from "Excellent," through to "Good," "Fair," "Poor,"or "Unsatisfactory." Some agencies will use a numeric score.

You will be provided with a copy of the agency's report as soon as possible after the evaluation is completed. You will be allowed at least 30 days to comment on the report, and, if necessary, refer the evaluation to a higher level. However, the agency makes the final decision.

Reports are completed annually during the life of the contract. The agency will keep copies of the report, as well as your response and comments, for a maximum of three years after the end of the contract.

Significant or recurring problems that may be included in the report might be such things as:

- Failing to perform the work in accordance with the terms of the contract.
- A history of repeated failure to perform, or an unsatisfactory performance.
- Violations of certain laws such as the Drug-Free Workplace Act or the Buy America Act.
- Unfair trade practices, a lack of integrity, or a failure to observe standard business ethical practices.

The Past Performance Information Retrieval System (PPIRS) is the site where federal agencies note how well you performed on any awarded contract. As stated previously, this information is shared among other agencies. You can have access to your own records, and may comment upon anything

in the report, but you do *not* have access to the records of other contractors. *www.ppirs.gov/*

VETERANS REPORTING REQUIREMENTS

Federal Acquisition Regulation (FAR) 52.222-35 forbids any form of discrimination against any veteran or disabled veteran. It applies to *all* employment openings (full-time, part-time, and temporary) *except* for:

- Executive and top management positions.
- Positions that will be filled from within your organization.
- Positions lasting three days or fewer.

Under the terms of this regulation you must list all your employment openings during the duration of the contract at an appropriate local public employment service office of the state (for example, at the U.S. Department of Labor's America's Job Bank). You must also post employment notices stating the employee's rights, your obligations and so on.

Any contractor or subcontractor who receives a federal government contract that is valued at $25,000 or greater must file the "Federal Contractor Veteran Employment Report" (VETS-100 Report) on an annual basis (FAR 52.222-37).

CHAPTER 8
STEPPING UP TO THE NEXT LEVEL

WHAT COMES NEXT?
AN OVERVIEW

In this chapter we discuss the larger sales opportunities that are available to you, once you have got your feet wet selling to the federal government, and you have determined that you are competitive in this marketplace. We discuss contracts such as Invitation for Bid and Request for Proposals (RFP) for both products and services.

GWACs

Government Wide Acquisition Contracts (GWACs) may offer you more sales opportunities, including the Department of Defense's "E-Mall" program. We'll explore some of these possibilities.

GSA Contracts

We'll also take a look at the General Services Administration's (GSA) Federal Supply Schedule Contract (also known as a GSA

Contract). The GSA's Schedules Program establishes long-term, government-wide contracts with commercial firms. These schedules give government purchasing agents access to more than 10 million commercial supplies and services. Agencies can order directly from GSA Schedule contractors, or through the GSA's online shopping and ordering system, called Advantage!

Government Wide Acquisition Contracts for Information Technology

Government Wide Acquisition Contracts, or GWACs, are Information Technology Services contracts that are established by the General Services Administration (GSA) and can be used by any f(ACES)Federal Government agency.

The General Service Administration has set up several GWAC programs:

- 8a STARS -Streamlined Technology Acquisition Resources for Services—for Information Technology small businesses who have been certified as 8a (Disadvantaged).
- Alliant and Alliant Small Business.
- ANSWER—Applications 'N Support for Widely-diverse End-user Requirements.
- HUB-Zone—for Information Technology businesses which are located in a Historically Underutilized Business Zone.
- ITOP 11 Information Technology Omnibus Procurement.
- Millennia and Millennia Lite.
- VETS—Veterans Technology Services—for Veteran-Owned Small Information Technology Businesses.

- ACES—Access Certificates for Electronic Services.
- Virtual Data Center Services.

THE GENERAL SERVICES ADMINISTRATION'S (GSA) FEDERAL SUPPLY SCHEDULE

The GSA's Schedules Program establishes long-term government-wide contracts with commercial firms. These schedules give government purchasing agents access to more than 10 million commercial supplies and services. These are ordered directly from GSA Schedule contractors, or through the *GSA Advantage!* online shopping and ordering system.

When you submit the paperwork in order to apply for a GSA Schedule contract you *must* give the government your best price—that is, you promise to give the government a price that is *at least* equal to that which you offer your Most Favored Customers.

In the GSA proposal, you tell the agency who you are, what you do, your terms and conditions, and your pricing structure. Because this is not a competitive bid, as long as the paperwork is submitted correctly, you will be awarded a contract.

This contract is Indefinite Delivery, Indefinite Quantity (IDIQ). This means there is no guarantee that they will purchase what you are proposing.

Once you are awarded a GSA contract number, it is the equivalent of an Approved Vendor Number—that is, it authorizes all purchasing agents from all agencies to purchase your product or service, and gives you exposure throughout this marketplace.

The GSA contract is valid for two years with three one-year options, followed by three five-year options. If you do not sell more than $25,000 in the first two years, your contract could be terminated. This is also true for every option year.

Once you are awarded a GSA Contract number, your products and services are posted on a government Website known as *GSA Advantage!*

OTHER GOVERNMENT WIDE ACQUISITION CONTRACTS

There are other agencies who have also established GWACs you may wish to look at:

- The Department of Commerce has a GWAC called **COMMITS**, or Commerce Information Technology Solutions. *http://oam.ocs.doc.gov/commits/index.html*

- **The Department of Defense E-Mall Program.** There are a few differences between the DOD E-Mall and the Federal Supply Schedule. The E-Mall allows all Department of Defense agencies to purchase from their own store. The term of the E-Mall contract is much shorter than the GSA's Contract. *www.dscc.dla.mil/programs/emall*

IN CONCLUSION

Now that you have more tools and better direction than most of your active competitors, there is no reason for you not to be successful in this marketplace, as long as you are aggressive.

One of the most common mistakes that a company makes is trying to pursue the largest customer in the entire world on a part-time basis. The work *never* gets done! The commitment of your time to this marketplace, as with anything else, will ensure your success. In this marketplace, it is more important to be aggressive than competitive. Submit as many offers as you possibly can to ensure that your company will be exposed in a positive light as an interested vendor.

I strongly urge that you treat government employees with the same amount of respect and professionalism that you treat your commercial prospects. You are doing business with highly trained professionals that are here to help you. Treat them accordingly.

When you are seriously considering submitting an offer, make sure that you stay well within the boundaries of your capabilities. It is better *not* to submit an offer, than have a contract withdrawn because you could not complete the project. Not only would this tarnish your reputation in this marketplace, but it could cost you cash penalties.

You do not have a great deal of competition in this marketplace. In many instances you will not be competing with the same company more than twice.

Remember: You are in the business of making a profit, *not* of being awarded a contract. If you cannot make a profit in this marketplace, then you don't need the government as your customer!

You are about to do business with the biggest and best customer in the entire world! There are a multitude of opportunities available to you every day.

Opportunities always arrive dressed in *working* clothes!

If you are willing to put in the time and commitment, you *will* reap the rewards!

APPENDIX

AN OVERVIEW

In the following pages you will find:

Central Contractor Registration (CCR) Worksheet. This worksheet allows you to understand the information that you will need to gather together about your company before you register at the Central Contractor's website.

Offeror's Representations and Certifications Applications Worksheet. We have provided you with a complete copy of the Offeror's Representations and Certifications document, so that you can understand the information you will need to provide when you register your company at the new ORCA Website.

U.S. Trade Agreement Acts Designated Countries. A "Designated Country" may be a Free Trade Agreement Country (NAFTA), a World Trade Organization

Government Procurement Agreement Country, a Least Developed Country, or a Caribbean Basin Country. Here we provide a consolidated list, along with their approved 2-digit codes.

Unit of Issue Codes. Although "ea" for "each" may be self-explanatory, at other times federal agencies may use other Unit of Issue codes which are not so intuitive! Here is a complete list of the Unit of Issue codes used by federal agencies.

CENTRAL CONTRACTOR REGISTRATION WORKSHEET

Use this worksheet to gather together the information you will need in order to register your company in CCR. Once you have all this information, go to the CCR Website at *www.ccr.gov* and register. You will need to update or renew your registration annually.

(M)= Mandatory

<u>General Information</u>

DUNS Number **(M)**: _____

CAGE Code **(M)**:_____

Legal Business Name **(M)**:_____

Doing Business As: _____

Tax ID **(M)**:_____**OR** Social Security Number:)_____

Division Name:_____ Division Number:_____

Corporate Web Page URL (Company Website address):_____

Physical Address **(M)**:_____

City **(M)**:_____ State **(M)**:_____

Zip/Postal Code **(M)**:_____ Zip Plus 4 **(M)**: _____

Country **(M)**:_____

Mailing Address **(M)**:_____If different from physical address

Business Name **(M)**:_____

Mailing Address (PO Box is acceptable) **(M)**:_____

City **(M)**:_____ State **(M)**:_____

Zip/Postal Code:_____Zip Plus 4 **(M)**:_____

Country **(M)**:_____

Business Start Date **(M)**(mm/dd/yyyy): _____

Number of Employees **(M)**:_____

Fiscal Year Close Date **(M)** (mm/dd):_____

Annual Revenue **(M)**:_____

Type of Organization (M):_____

Corporate Entity (Not Tax Exempt)

Corporate Entity (Tax Exempt)

State of Incorporation **(M)**:_____or Country (if other than US):____

Sole Proprietorship

Partnership

U.S. Government Entity

Federal _____State _____Local_____

Foreign Government

International Organization

Other

Owner Information (M) if Sole Proprietorship:

Name:_____

U.S. Phone:_____Ext.:_____

Non U.S. Phone:_____Ext:_____

Fax (U.S. Only):_____

E-mail:_____

Business Type(s) (M) Check all that apply:

8(a) Program Participant (also check small business)

American Indian Owned

Hub Zone Business (also check small business)

Minority Owned Business (Must choose one below):

        Subcontinent Asian (Asian-Indian) American

        Asian-Pacific American

        Black American

        Hispanic American

        Native American

        No Representation/None of the above

  Large Business

  Small Business

  Small Disadvantaged Business (also check small business)

  Woman Owned Business

  Veteran Owned Business

  Service Disabled Veteran Owned

Construction Firm

Educational Institution

Emerging Small Business

Foreign Supplier

Historically Black College/Univ.

Labor Surplus Area Firm

Limited Liability Company

Manufacturer of Goods

Minority Institution

Municipality

Nonprofit Institution

Research Institute

S Corporation

Service Location

Sheltered Workshop (JWOD)

Tribal Government

Party Performing Certification

Mandatory if approved for 8(a) certification through the Small Business Administration

Certifier's Name:_____

Address:_____

City:_____

State: _____ Zip/Postal Code:_____

Country: _____

Goods and Services:

NAICS Codes (M) North American Industrial Classification Code to identify what product or service your business provides (6 digit numeric). Search on *www.census.gov/epcd/www/naics.html.*

NAICS Code:_____

NAICS Code:_____

NAICS Code:_____

NAICS Code:_____

NAICS Code:_____

NAICS Code:_____

SIC Codes (M) Standard Industrial Classification Codes identify what type of activity your business performs (4 or 8 digit numeric). Search on *www.osha.gov/oshstats/sicser.html.*

SIC Code:_____

SIC Code:_____

SIC Code:_____

SIC Code:_____

SIC Code:_____

Financial Information:_____

Financial Institution Name:_____

(Bank name for Electronic Funds Transfer)   (If Non-US business, EFT is optional)

ABA Routing Number **(M)** (9digits):_____

Must indicate type of account **(M)**

Account Number **(M)**:_____ Checking OR Savings

Lockbox Number:

Automated Clearing House (**M**) at least one method of contact must be entered

ACH U.S. Phone Number:_____

ACH Fax (U.S. Only):_____

ACH Non-U.S. Phone:_____

ACH Email:_____

Remittance Address (M):

Business Name (**M**):_____

Address (**M**):_____

City (**M**):_____ State (**M**):_____ Zip/Postal Code (**M**):_____

Country (**M**):_____

Accounts Receivable Contact (M):

Name (**M**):_____

E-mail (**M**):_____

U.S. Phone (**M**): _____ Ext.:_____

Non U.S. Phone:_____ Ext.:_____

Fax (U.S. Only):_____

Do you (the Registrant) use or accept Credit Cards as a method of Purchase or Payment? (**M**).   Yes   No

Point of Contact Information:

CCR Point of Contact (M)

Name:_____

E-mail:_____

U.S. Phone:_____ Ext.:_____

Non U.S. Phone:_____ Ext.:_____

Fax (U.S. Only):_____

CCR Alternate Point of Contact (M)

Name:_____

E-mail:_____

U.S. Phone:_____ Ext.:____

Non U.S. Phone:_____Ext.:_____

Fax (U.S. Only): _____

You may list two people for each of these following positions if you wish:_____

Government Business Point of Contact

Name:_____

E-mail:_____

Address: _____

City:_____ State:_____ Zip Code:_____

U.S. Phone: _____Ext.: _____

Non U.S. Phone:_____ Ext.:_____

Fax (U.S. Only):_____

Government Business Point of Contact Alternate

Name:_____

E-mail:_____

Address:_____

City:_____State:_____ Zip Code:_____

U.S. Phone:_____ Ext.:_____

Non U.S. Phone:_____ Ext.:_____

Fax (U.S. Only):_____

Electronic Business Point of Contact (M)

Name: _____

E-mail: _____

Address:_____

City:_____State:_____Zip Code:_____

U.S. Phone:_____Ext.:_____

Non U.S. Phone:_____ Ext.:_____

Fax (U.S. Only):_____

Name **(M)**:_____

Electronic Business Point of Contact Alternate (M)

Name:_____

E-mail:_____

Address:_____

City:_____ State:_____ Zip Code: _____

U.S. Phone:_____ Ext.: _____

Non U.S. Phone: _____ Ext.:_____

Fax (U.S. Only):_____

Past Performance Point of Contact

Name:_____

E-mail:_____

Address:_____

City:_____ State:_____ Zip Code:_____

U.S. Phone:_____ Ext.:_____

Non U.S. Phone:_____ Ext.:_____

Fax (U.S. Only):_____

Past Performance Point of Contact Alternate

Name:_____

E-mail:_____

Address:_____

City:_____ State:_____ Zip Code: _____

U.S. Phone: _____ Ext.: _____

Non U.S. Phone: _____ Ext.:_____

Fax (U.S. Only): _____

Marketing Partner ID (MPIN) _____

Offeror Representations and Certifications Applications Worksheet(FAR 52.212-3)

As stated throughout the previous chapters, starting in 2005, this section may now be completed online at the Offeror Representations and Certifications Application (ORCA) Website, via the Business Partner Network.

The ORCA Website address is: *http://orca.bpn.gov.*

Your first task will be to register for an MPIN (Marketing Partner Identification Number) at the Central Contractor Registration (CCR) Website.

Your MPIN number takes about 48 hours to appear in the system.

Once you have this information you can login into the ORCA Website to complete the online application.

Here is the full text of the regulation. Read carefully through the next section in order to fully understand what information you will need to gather together before you begin your registration at the site.

52.212-3—Offeror Representations and Certifications—Commercial Items.

As prescribed in 12.301(b)(2), insert the following provision:

Offeror Representations and Certifications—Commercial Items (June 2003)

(a) *Definitions.* As used in this provision:

"Emerging small business" means a small business concern whose size is no greater than 50 percent of the numerical size standard for the NAICS code designated.

"Forced or indentured child labor" means all work or service-

(1) Exacted from any person under the age of 18 under the menace of any penalty for its nonperformance and for which the worker does not offer himself voluntarily; or

(2) Performed by any person under the age of 18 pursuant to a contract the enforcement of which can be accomplished by process or penalties.

"Service-disabled veteran-owned small business concern"—

(1) Means a small business concern —

(i) Not less than 51 percent of which is owned by one or more service-disabled veterans or, in the case of any publicly owned business, not less than 51 percent of the stock of which is owned by one or more service-disabled veterans; and

(ii) The management and daily business operations of which are controlled by one or more service-disabled veterans or, in the case of a veteran with permanent and severe disability, the spouse or permanent caregiver of such veteran.(2) Service-disabled veteran means a veteran, as defined in 38 U.S.C. 101(2), with a disability that is service-connected, as defined in 38 U.S.C. 101(16).

"Small business concern" means a concern, including its affiliates, that is independently owned and operated, not dominant in the field of operation in which it is bidding on Government contracts, and qualified as a small business under the criteria in 13 CFR Part 121 and size standards in this solicitation.

"Veteran-owned small business concern" means a small business concern"—

(1) Not less than 51 percent of which is owned by one or more veterans(as defined at 38 U.S.C. 101(2)) or, in the case of any publicly owned business, not less than 51 percent of the stock of which is owned by one or more veterans; and

(2) The management and daily business operations of which are controlled by one or more veterans.

"Women-owned business concern" means a concern which is at least 51 percent owned by one or more women; or in the case of any publicly owned business, at least 51 percent of the its stock is owned by one or more women; and whose management and daily business operations are controlled by one or more women.

"Women-owned small business concern" means a small business concern —

(1) That is at least 51 percent owned by one or more women or, in the case of any publicly owned business, at least 51 percent of the stock of which is owned by one or more women; and

(2) Whose management and daily business operations are controlled by one or more women.

(b) *Taxpayer identification number (TIN) (26 U.S.C. 6109, 31 U.S.C. 7701).* (Not applicable if the offeror is required to provide this information to a central contractor registration database to be eligible for award.)

(1) All offerors must submit the information required in paragraphs (b)(3) through (b)(5) of this provision to comply with debt collection requirements of 31 U.S.C. 7701(c) and 3325(d), reporting requirements of 26 U.S.C. 6041, 6041A, and 6050M, and implementing regulations issued by the Internal Revenue Service (IRS).

(2) The TIN may be used by the government to collect and report on any delinquent amounts arising out of the offeror's relationship with the Government (31 U.S.C. 7701(c)(3)). If the resulting contract is subject to the payment reporting requirements described in FAR 4.904, the TIN provided hereunder may be matched with IRS records to verify the accuracy of the offeror's TIN.]

(3) *Taxpayer Identification Number (TIN).*

    * TIN:_____.

    * TIN has been applied for.

    * TIN is not required because:

* Offeror is a nonresident alien, foreign corporation, or foreign partnership that does not have income effectively connected with the conduct of a trade or business in the United States and does not have an office or place of business or a fiscal paying agent in the United States;

* Offeror is an agency or instrumentality of a foreign government;

* Offeror is an agency or instrumentality of the Federal Government;

(4) *Type of organization.*

* Sole proprietorship;

* Partnership;

* Corporate entity (not tax-exempt);

* Corporate entity (tax-exempt);

* Government entity (Federal, State, or local);

* Foreign government;

* International organization per 26 CFR 1.6049-4;

* Other_____.

(5) *Common parent.*

* Offeror is not owned or controlled by a common parent:

* Name and TIN of common parent:

    Name_____

    TIN_____

(c) Offerors must complete the following representations when the resulting contract is to be performed in the United States or its outlying areas. Check all that apply.

(1) *Small business concern.* The offeror represents as part of its offer that it * is, * is not a small business concern.

(2) *Veteran-owned small business concern.* [*Complete only if the offeror represented itself as a small business concern in paragraph (c)(1) of this provision.*] The offeror represents as part of its offer that it * is, * is not a veteran-owned small business concern.

(3) *Service-disabled veteran-owned small business concern.* [*Complete only if the offeror represented itself as a veteran-owned small business concern in paragraph (c)(2) of this provision.*] The offeror represents as part of its offer that it * is, * is not a service-disabled veteran-owned small business concern.

(4) *Small disadvantaged business concern.* [*Complete only if the offeror represented itself as a small business concern in paragraph (c)(1) of this provision.*] The offeror represents, for general statistical purposes, that it * is, * is not, a small disadvantaged business concern as defined in 13 CFR 124.1002.

(5) *Women-owned small business concern.* [*Complete only if the offeror represented itself as a small business concern in paragraph (c)(1) of this provision.*] The offeror represents that it * is, * is not a women-owned small business concern.

Note: Complete paragraphs (c)(6) and (c)(7) only if this solicitation is expected to exceed the simplified acquisition threshold.

(6) *Women-owned business concern (other than small business concern).* [*Complete only if the offeror is a*

women-owned business concern and did not represent itself as a small business concern in paragraph (c)(1) of this provision.]. The offeror represents that it * is, a women-owned business concern.

(7) *Tie bid priority for labor surplus area concerns.* If this is an invitation for bid, small business offerors may identify the labor surplus areas in which costs to be incurred on account of manufacturing or production (by offeror or first-tier subcontractors) amount to more than 50 percent of the contract price:_____

(8) Small Business Size for the Small Business Competitiveness Demonstration Program and for the Targeted Industry Categories under the Small Business Competitiveness Demonstration Program. *[Complete only if the offeror has represented itself to be a small business concern under the size standards for this solicitation.]*

(i) *[Complete only for solicitations indicated in an addendum as being set-aside for emerging small businesses in one of the four designated industry groups (DIGs).]* The offeror represents as part of its offer that it * is, * is not an emerging small business.

(ii) *[Complete only for solicitations indicated in an addendum as being for one of the targeted industry categories (TICs) or four designated industry groups (DIGs).]* Offeror represents as follows:

(A) Offeror's number of employees for the past 12 months (check the Employees column if size standard stated in the solicitation is expressed in terms of number of employees); or

(B) Offeror's average annual gross revenue for the last 3 fiscal years (check the Average Annual Gross Number of Revenues column if size standard stated in the solicitation is expressed in terms of annual receipts).

(Check one of the following):

Number of Employees	Average Annual Gross Revenues
50 or fewer	$1 million or less
51-100	$1,000,001-$2 million
101-250	$2,000,001-$3.5 million
251-500	$3,500,001-$5 million
501-750	$5,000,001-$10 million
751-1,000	$10,000,001-$17 million
Over 1,000	Over $17 million

(9) [*Complete only if the solicitation contains the clause at FAR 52.219-23, Notice of Price Evaluation Adjustment for Small Disadvantaged Business Concerns, or FAR 52.219-25, Small Disadvantaged Business Participation Program-Disadvantaged Status and Reporting, and the offeror desires a benefit based on its disadvantaged status.*]

(i) *General.* The offeror represents that either-

(A) It * is, * is not certified by the Small Business Administration as a small disadvantaged business concern and identified, on the date of this representation, as a certified small disadvantaged business concern in the database maintained by the Small Business Administration (PRO-Net), and that no material change in disadvantaged ownership and control has occurred since its certification, and, where the concern is owned by one or more individuals claiming disadvantaged status, the net worth of each individual upon whom the certification is based does not exceed $750,000 after taking into account the applicable exclusions set forth at 13 CFR 124.104(c)(2); or

(B) It *has, * has not submitted a completed application to the Small Business Administration or a Private Certifier to be certified as a small disadvantaged business concern in accordance with 13 CFR 124, Subpart B, and a decision on that application is pending, and that no material change in disadvantaged ownership and control has occurred since its application was submitted.

(ii) *Joint Ventures under the Price Evaluation Adjustment for Small Disadvantaged Business Concerns.* The offeror represents, as part of its offer, that it is a joint venture that complies with the requirements in 13 CFR 124.1002(f) and that the representation in paragraph (c)(9)(i) of this provision is accurate for the small disadvantaged business concern that is participating in the joint venture. [*The offeror shall enter the name of the small disadvantaged business concern that is participating in the joint venture:* _____.]

(10) *HUBZone small business concern.* [*Complete only if the offeror represented itself as a small business concern in paragraph (c)(1) of this provision.*] The offeror represents, as part of its offer, that—

(i) It * is, * is not a HUBZone small business concern listed, on the date of this representation, on the List of Qualified HUBZone Small Business Concerns maintained by the Small Business Administration, and no material change in ownership and control, principal office, or HUBZone employee percentage has occurred since it was certified by the Small Business Administration in accordance with 13 CFR part 126; and

(ii) It * is, * not a joint venture that complies with the requirements of 13 CFR part 126, and the representation in paragraph (c)(10)(i) of this provision is accurate for the HUBZone small business concern or concerns that are participating in the joint venture. [*The offeror shall enter the name or names of the HUBZone small business concern or concerns that are participating in the joint venture*:_____.] Each HUBZone small business concern participating in the joint venture shall submit a separate signed copy of the HUBZone representation.

(d) *Representations required to implement provisions of Executive Order 11246 —*

(1) Previous contracts and compliance. The offeror represents that —

(i) It * has, * has not, participated in a previous contract or subcontract subject to the Equal Opportunity clause of this solicitation; and

(ii) It * has, * has not, filed all required compliance reports.

(2) *Affirmative Action Compliance.* The offeror represents that —

(i) It * has developed and has on file, * has not developed and does not have on file, at each establishment, affirmative action programs required by rules and regulations of the Secretary of Labor (41 CFR parts 60-1 and 60-2), or

(ii) It * has not previously had contracts subject to the written affirmative action programs requirement of the rules and regulations of the Secretary of Labor.

(e) *Certification Regarding Payments to Influence Federal Transactions (31 U.S.C. 1352).* (Applies only if the contract is expected to exceed $100,000.) By submission of its offer, the offeror certifies to the best of its knowledge and belief that no Federal appropriated funds have been paid or will be paid to any person for influencing or attempting to influence an officer or employee of any agency, a Member of Congress, an officer or employee of Congress or an employee of a Member of Congress on his or her behalf in connection with the award of any resultant contract.

(f) *Buy American Act Certificate.* (Applies only if the clause at Federal Acquisition Regulation (FAR) 52.225-1, Buy American Act - Supplies, is included in this solicitation.)

(1) The offeror certifies that each end product, except those listed in paragraph (f)(2) of this provision, is a domestic end product and that the offeror has considered components of unknown origin to have been mined, produced, or manufactured outside the United States. The offeror shall list as foreign end products those end products manufactured in the United States that do not qualify as domestic end products. The terms "component," "domestic end product," "end product," "foreign end product," and "United States" are defined in the clause of this solicitation entitled "Buy American Act-Supplies."

(2) Foreign End Products:

LINE ITEM NO.	COUNTRY OF ORIGIN

[*List as necessary*]

(3) The Government will evaluate offers in accordance with the policies and procedures of FAR Part 25.

(g)

(1) *Buy American Act — North American Free Trade Agreement — Israeli Trade Act Certificate.* (Applies only if the clause at FAR 52.225-3, Buy American Act — North American Free Trade Agreement — Israeli Trade Act, is included in this solicitation.)

(i) The offeror certifies that each end product, except those listed in paragraph (g)(1)(ii) or (g)(1)(iii) of this provision, is a domestic end product and that the offeror has considered components of unknown origin to have been mined, produced, or manufactured outside the United States. The terms "component," "domestic end product," "end product," "foreign end product," and "United States" are defined in the clause of this solicitation entitled "Buy American Act-North American Free Trade Agreement-Israeli Trade Act."

(ii) The offeror certifies that the following supplies are NAFTA country end products or Israeli end products as defined in the clause of this solicitation entitled "Buy American Act-North American Free Trade Agreement-Israeli Trade Act":

NAFTA Country or Israeli End Products:

LINE ITEM NO.	COUNTRY OF ORIGIN

[*List as necessary*]

(iii) The offeror shall list those supplies that are foreign end products (other than those listed in paragraph (g)(1)(ii) or this provision) as defined in the clause of this solicitation entitled "Buy American Act-North American Free Trade Agreement-Israeli Trade Act." The offeror shall list as other foreign end products those end products manufactured in the United States that do not qualify as domestic end products.

Other Foreign End Products:

LINE ITEM NO.	COUNTRY OF ORIGIN

[List as necessary]

(iv) The Government will evaluate offers in accordance with the policies and procedures of FAR Part 25.

(2) *Buy American Act-North American Free Trade Agreements-Israeli Trade Act Certificate, Alternate I (May 2002).* If Alternate I to the clause at FAR 52.225-3 is included in this solicitation, substitute the following paragraph (g)(1)(ii) for paragraph (g)(1)(ii) of the basic provision:

(g)(1)(ii) The offeror certifies that the following supplies are Canadian end products as defined in the clause of this solicitation entitled "Buy American Act-North American Free Trade Agreement-Israeli Trade Act":

Canadian End Products:

Line Item No.:

_____

[List as necessary]

(3) *Buy American Act-North American Free Trade Agreements-Israeli Trade Act Certificate, Alternate II (May 2002).* If Alternate II to the clause at FAR 52.225-3 is included in this solicitation, substitute the following paragraph (g)(1)(ii) for paragraph (g)(1)(ii) of the basic provision:

(g)(1)(ii) The offeror certifies that the following supplies are Canadian end products or Israeli end products as defined in the clause of this solicitation entitled "Buy American Act—North American Free Trade Agreement—Israeli Trade Act":

Canadian or Israeli End Products:

LINE ITEM NO.	COUNTRY OF ORIGIN

[*List as necessary*]

(4) *Trade Agreements Certificate.* (Applies only if the clause at FAR 52.225-5, Trade Agreements, is included in this solicitation.)

(i) The offeror certifies that each end product, except those listed in paragraph (g)(4)(ii) of this provision, is a U.S.-made, designated country, Caribbean Basin country, or NAFTA country end product, as defined in the clause of this solicitation entitled "Trade Agreements."

(ii) The offeror shall list as other end products those end products that are not U.S.-made, designated country, Caribbean Basin country, or NAFTA country end products.

Other End Products

LINE ITEM NO.	COUNTRY OF ORIGIN

[*List as necessary*]

> (iii) The Government will evaluate offers in accordance with the policies and procedures of FAR Part 25. For line items subject to the Trade Agreements Act, the Government will evaluate offers of U.S.-made, designated country, Caribbean Basin country, or NAFTA country end products without regard to the restrictions of the Buy American Act. The Government will consider for award only offers of U.S.-made, designated country, Caribbean Basin country, or NAFTA country end products unless the Contracting Officer determines that there are no offers for such products or that the offers for such products are insufficient to fulfill the requirements of the solicitation.

(h) *Certification Regarding Debarment, Suspension or Ineligibility for Award (Executive Order 12549).* (Applies only if the contract value is expected to exceed the simplified acquisition threshold.) The offeror certifies, to the best of its knowledge and belief, that the offeror and/or any of its principals—

> (1) * Are, * are not presently debarred, suspended, proposed for debarment, or declared ineligible for the award of contracts by any Federal agency; and

> (2) * Have, * have not, within a three-year period preceding this offer, been convicted of or had a civil judgment rendered against them for: commission of fraud or a criminal offense in connection with obtaining, attempting to obtain, or

performing a Federal, state or local government contract or subcontract; violation of Federal or state antitrust statutes relating to the submission of offers; or commission of embezzlement, theft, forgery, bribery, falsification or destruction of records, making false statements, tax evasion, or receiving stolen property; and

(3) * Are, * are not presently indicted for, or otherwise criminally or civilly charged by a Government entity with, commission of any of these offenses.

(i) *Certification Regarding Knowledge of Child Labor for Listed End Products (Executive Order 13126). [The Contracting Officer must list in paragraph (i)(1) any end products being acquired under this solicitation that are included in the List of Products Requiring Contractor Certification as to Forced or Indentured Child Labor, unless excluded at 22.1503(b).]*

(1) Listed End Product

Listed End Product	Listed Country of Origin

(2) *Certification. [If the Contracting Officer has identified end products and countries of origin in paragraph (i)(1) of this provision, then the offeror must certify to either (i)(2)(i) or (i)(2)(ii) by checking the appropriate block.]*

[ ] (i) The offeror will not supply any end product listed in paragraph (i)(1) of this provision that was mined, produced, or manufactured in the corresponding country as listed for that product.

[ ] (ii) The offeror may supply an end product listed in paragraph (i)(1) of this provision that was mined, produced, or manufactured in the corresponding

country as listed for that product. The offeror certifies that is has made a good faith effort to determine whether forced or indentured child labor was used to mine, produce, or manufacture any such end product furnished under this contract. On the basis of those efforts, the offeror certifies that it is not aware of any such use of child labor.

(End of Provision)

Alternate I (*Apr 2002*). As prescribed in 12.301(b)(2), add the following paragraph (c)(11) to the basic provision:

(11) (Complete if the offeror has represented itself as disadvantaged in paragraph (c)(4) or (c)(9) of this provision.) [*The offeror shall check the category in which its ownership falls*]:

____Black American.

____Hispanic American.

____Native American (American Indians, Eskimos, Aleuts, or Native Hawaiians).

____Asian-Pacific American (persons with origins from Burma, Thailand, Malaysia, Indonesia, Singapore, Brunei, Japan, China, Taiwan, Laos, Cambodia (Kampuchea), Vietnam, Korea, The Philippines, U.S. Trust Territory or the Pacific Islands (Republic of Palau), Republic of the Marshall Islands, Federated States of Micronesia, the Commonwealth of the Northern Mariana Islands, Guam, Samoa, Macao, Hong Kong, Fiji, Tonga, Kiribati, Tuvalu, or Nauru).

____Subcontinent Asian (Asian-Indian) American (persons with origins from India, Pakistan, Bangladesh, Sri Lanka, Bhutan, the Maldives Islands, or Nepal).

____Individual/concern, other than one of the preceding.

Alternate II (*Oct 2000*). As prescribed in 12.301(b)(2), add the following paragraph (c)(9)(iii) to the basic provision:

(iii) Address. The offeror represents that its address ___is, ___ is not in a region for which a small disadvantaged business procurement mechanism is authorized and its address has not changed since its certification as a small disadvantaged business concern or submission of its application for certification. The list of authorized small disadvantaged business procurement mechanisms and regions is posted at http://www.arnet.gov/References/sdbadjustments.htm. The offeror shall use the list in effect on the date of this solicitation. "Address," as used in this provision, means the address of the offeror as listed on the Small Business Administration's register of small disadvantaged business concerns or the address on the completed application that the concern has submitted to the Small Business Administration or a Private Certifier in accordance with 13 CFR part 124, subpart B. For joint ventures, "address" refers to the address of the small disadvantaged business concern that is participating in the joint venture.

U.S. TRADE AGREEMENTS ACT, DESIGNATED COUNTRIES

The following pages contain a consolidated list of the federal government's designated countries, as per the Trade Agreements Act, and the corresponding government-approved 2-digit codes which may be used for those countries.

The following Website contains a list of two digit codes that may be used by manufacturers to designate the country of origin:

www.iana.org/cctld/cctld-whois.htm.

A Designated Country may mean:

    1) A World Trade Organization Government Procurement Agreement Country.

    2) A Free Trade Agreement Country.

3) A Least Developed Country.

4) A Caribbean Basin Country.

Designated	Designation	2-digit code
Afghanistan	Least Developed	AF
Angola	Least Developed	AO
Antigua & Barbuda	Caribbean Basin	AG
Antilles, Netherlands	Caribbean Basin	AN
Aruba	Caribbean Basin	AW
Australia	Free Trade Agreement	AU
Austria	World Trade Organization	AT
Bahamas	Caribbean Basin	BS
Bangladesh	Least Developed	BD
Barbados	Caribbean Basin	BB
Belgium	World Trade Organization	BE
Belize	Caribbean Basin	BZ
Benin	Least Developed	BJ
Bhutan	Least Developed	BT
Burkina Faso	Least Developed	BF
Burundi	Least Developed	BI
Cambodia	Least Developed	KH
Canada	World Trade Org/Free Trade Agreement	CA
Cape Verde	Least Developed	CV
Central African Republic	Least Developed	CF
Chad	Least Developed	TD
Chile	Free Trade Agreement	CL
Congo, Democratic Rep	Least Developed	CD
Cormoros	Least Developed	KM
Costa Rica	Caribbean Basin	CR
Cyprus	World Trade Organization	CY

Czech Republic	World Trade Organization	CZ
Denmark	World Trade Organization	DK
Djibouti	Least Developed	DJ
Dominica	Caribbean Basin	DM
Dominican Republic	Caribbean Basin	DO
East Timor	Least Developed	TP
El Salvador	Caribbean Basin	SV
Equatorial Guinea	Least Developed	GN
Eritrea	Least Developed	ER
Estonia	World Trade Organization	EE
Ethiopia	Least Developed	ET
Finland	World Trade Organization	FI
France	World Trade Organization	FR
Gambia	Least Developed	GM
Germany	World Trade Organization	DE
Greece	World Trade Organization	GR
Grenada	Caribbean Basin	GD
Guatemala	Caribbean Basin	GT
Guyana	Caribbean Basin	GY
Guinea	Least Developed	GG
Guinea-Bissau	Least Developed	GW
Haiti	Least Developed	HT
Honduras	Caribbean Basin	HN
Hong Kong	World Trade Organization	HK
Hungary	World Trade Organization	HU
Iceland	World Trade Organization	IS
Ireland	World Trade Organization	IE
Israel	World Trade Organization	IL
Italy	World Trade Organization	IT
Jamaica	Caribbean Basin	JM

Japan	World Trade Organization	JP
Kiribati	Least Developed	KI
Korea (Republic)	World Trade Organization	KR
Latvia	World Trade Organization	LV
Laos	Least Developed	LA
Lesotho	Least Developed	LS
Liechtenstein	World Trade Organization	LI
Lithuania	World Trade Organization	LT
Luxemborg	World Trade Organization	LU
Madagascar	Least Developed	MG
Malawi	Least Developed	MW
Maldives	Least Developed	MV
Mali	Least Developed	ML
Malta	World Trade Organization	MT
Mauritania	Least Developed	MR
Mexico	Free Trade Agreement	MX
Montserrat	Caribbean Basin	MS
Morocco	Free Trade Agreement	MA
Mozambique	Least Developed	MZ
Nepal	Least Developed	NP
Netherlands	World Trade Organization	NL
Nicaragua	Caribbean Basin	NI
Niger	Least Developed	NE
Norway	World Trade Organization	NO
Poland	World Trade Organization	PL
Portugal	World Trade Organization	PT
Rwanda	Least Developed	RW
Samoa, Western	Least Developed	WS
Sao Tome & Principe	Least Developed	ST
Senegal	Least Developed	SN

Sierra Leone	Least Developed	SL
Singapore	Free Trade Agreement	SG
Slovak Republic	World Trade Organization	SK
Slovenia	World Trade Organization	SI
Solomon Islands	Least Developed	SB
Somalia	Least Developed	SO
Spain	World Trade Organization	ES
St Kitts & Nevis	Caribbean Basin	KN
St Lucia	Caribbean Basin	LC
St Vincent & Grenadines	Caribbean Basin	VC
Sweden	World Trade Organization	SE
Switzerland	World Trade Organization	CH
Tanzania	Least Developed	TZ
Togo	Least Developed	TG
Trinidad & Tobago	Caribbean Basin	TT
Tuvalu	Least Developed	TV
Uganda	Least Developed	UG
United Kingdom	World Trade Organization	UK/GB
Vanatu	Least Developed	VU
Virgin Islands, British	Caribbean Basin	VG
Yemen	Least Developed	YE
Zambia	Least Developed	ZM

UNIT OF ISSUE CODES

AM	Ampoule	CZ	Cubic Meter	JR	Jar	RD	Round
AT	Assortment	DC	Decagram	KG	Kilogram	RL	Reel
AY	Assembly	DE	Decimeter	KM	Kilometer	RM	Ream
BA	Ball	DG	Decigram	KR	Carat	RO	Roll
BD	Bundle	DL	Deciliter	KT	Kit	RX	Thousand Rounds
BE	Bale	DM	Dram	LB	Pound	SD	Skid
BF	Board Foot	DR	Drum	LF	Linear Foot	SE	Set
BG	Bag	DW	Pennyweight	LG	Length	SF	Square Foot
BK	Book	DZ	Dozen	LI	Liter	SH	Sheet
BL	Barrel	EA	Each	LI	Liter Thousand	SI	Square Inch
BO	Bolt	EX	Exposure	MC	Cubic	SK	Skein
BQ	Briquet	FD	Fold	MC	Thousand	SL	Spool
BR	Bar	FR	Frame	ME	Meal	SM	Square Meter
BT	Bottle	FT	Foot	MF	Thousand Feet	SO	Shot
BX	Box	FV	Five	MG	Milligram	SP	Strip
CA	Cartridge	FY	Fifty	MI	Mile	SQ	Square
CB	Carboy Cubic	GG	Great Gross	ML	Milliliter	SX	Stick
CC	Centimeter	GI	Gill	MM	Millimeter	SY	Square Yard
CD	Cubic Yard	GL	Gallon	MR	Meter	TD	Twenty-four
CE	Cone	GM	Gram	MX	Thousand	TE	Ten
CF	Cubic Foot	GN	Grain	OT	Outfit	TF	Twenty-five
CG	Centigram	GP	Group	OZ	Ounce	TN	Ton (2,000 lb)
CI	Cubic Inch	GR	Gross	PD	Pad	TO	Troy Ounce
CK	Cake	HD	Hundred	PG	Package	TS	Thirty-six
CL	Coil	HF	Hundred Feet	PI	Pillow	TT	Tablet
CM	Centimeter	HK	Hank	PM	Plate	TU	Tube
CN	Can	HP	Hundred Pounds	PR	Pair	US	U.S.P. Unit
CO	Container	HS	Hundred Square	PT	Pint	VI	Vial
CU	Curie	HW	Hundred Weight	PX	Pellet	YD	Yard
CY	Cylinder	HY	Hundred Yards	PZ	Packet		
RA	Ration	IN	Inch	QT	Quart		

INDEX

A

A-76 competition, 176
AbiWeb, 104
Acceptance, 185
ACES, 195
Acquisition Center for Excellence Services, 177
Acquisition Streamlining and Standardization Information Systems (ASSIST), 124-125, 158, 183
Adjectival rating, 174-175
Affirmative action laws, 154
Amendments, 50-51, 71-73
America's Job Bank, 192
American National Standards Institute, 125
American Society for Testing and Material, 179, 183
ANSWER, 194
Army Single Face to Industry, 126
Auto-IDPOs, 96, 99, 101
Automated Best Value System, 69-70, 93, 101-102

B

Bar codes, 181
Batch Quoting, 115
Best Value Purchasing, 33
Bids without Exception, 99
Breach of contract, 190-191
Business codes, 36
Business Partner Network, 89, 206
Business System Modernization, 101
Buy American Act, 155, 216-220
Buyer codes, 122

C

Central Contractors Registration (CCR), 28, 38-39, 41, 42, 44, 45, 155, 187

Central Contractors Registration Worksheet, 199, 200-206

cFolders, 94, 102, 124

Child labor laws, 154, 221

Class I Ozone-Depleting Substances (CIODS), 158

Clean Air Act, 158

Code of Federal Regulations, 172

Commercial and Government Entity (CAGE) codes, 40-41, 115-116, 121, 166, 182, 186

Commercial over-the-counter items, 35

Commercial packaging, 144, 179, 180

COMMITS, 196

Commodity Line Item Number, 142

COMPARE, 177

Competitive Sourcing Program, 176

Consolidated Purchasing Programs, 33

Contract Clauses, 148-156

Contract Performance Monitoring, 190

Contract Work Hours and Safety Standards Act, 171

Contract, breach of, 190-191

Contract, fulfilling the terms of your, 179-192

Convict labor laws, 154

Copeland "Anti-Kickback" Act, 171

Cost Accounting Standards Notices and Certification Clause, 157

D

Data Universal Numbering System (DUNS), 36, 44

Date range, 121, 122

Davis Bacon Act, 171

Defense Federal Acquisition Regulations Supplements, 101, 126

Defense Finance and Accounting Service (DFAS), 186

Defense Logistics Agency, 43, 69, 94, 97, 124, 144, 183

Defense Logistics Information Service, 41

Defense Priorities and Allocations System, 138, 159

Defense Supply Centers, 55, 97, 101, 104, 181

Delays, excusable, 153

Department of Defense E-Mall Program, 196

Department of Defense Single Stock Point, 158

Designated Countries, 199, 223-227

DIBBS Website, 55-56, 69, 93-116, 117, 155

Distributing Date Report (DD250), 183-184

DLA Distribution Depot, 181

Drawing Distribution Codes, 102-103

Drawings, 102-105

Dun & Bradstreet, 36, 150

DUNS, 166

E

8a STARS, 194

Electronic Business Point of Contact, 187

Electronic Data Interchange (EDI), 188

Electronic Document Access, 188

Electronic Funds Transfer, 155

Electronic Quoting System, 135, 146

E-Mall, 196

Employer Identification Number, 37

Environmental Attribute Codes, 106

Environmental Technologies Opportunities Portal, 107

Environmentally Preferable Purchasing, 107

Equal-opportunity laws, 154

Evaluation factors, 173

Excusable delays, 153

F

FarSite, 158

Fast Award bids, 96

FedBid, 34-36

FedBizOpps, 43, 47-92, 130, 131

Federal Acquisition Regulations, 82-89, 101, 120

Federal Acquisition Streamlining Act, 32

Federal Agency Business Forecasts, 90

Federal Assets Sales, 90

Federal Bureau of Prisons, 130

Federal Contractor Veteran Employment Report, 192

Federal Emergency Management Agency, 92

Federal Energy Management Program, 107

Federal Grants, 90

Federal Prison Industries, 68, 129-130

Federal Procurement Data Center, 132

Federal Standard Forms, 135-163

Federal Stock Class, 120-121, 125

Federal Supply Classification (FSC) Codes, 42-43, 50, 53, 91, 95, 100, 126

Federal Travel Regulations (FTR), 172

FedTeds, 91

Firm Fixed Price, 142, 159

First Article Testing, 56

Foreign Trade Data System, 132

Freight on Board, 138, 146, 153

Fulfilling the terms of your contract, 179-192

G

General Services Administration (GSA), 38, 92, 108, 128, 172, 193-194

General Services Administration Schedule contracts, 27, 34, 35

General Services Administration's Federal Supply Schedule, 195-196

Government Printing Office, 132

Government Wide Acquisition Contracts (GWACs), 27, 33, 194-195

Green Procurement Program, 106

GSA Advantage!, 195

H

H2 Manual, 42

Higher-Level Contract Quality Requirement, 185

HUB-Zones, 77, 194, 214

Hurricane and Disaster Contracting, 91-92

I

Inland Revenue Service, 37-38
Inspection, 184-185
Insurance, 172
Integrated Acquisition
    Environment, 90
Internet Quoting System, 117
Invitation for Bid, 32
Invoicing, 186-189
Israeli Trade Act, 217-220

J

Jarvits Wagner O'Day Program,
    67-68
Joint Travel Regulations (JTR), 172

L

Labor laws, 154, 155-156
Liability insurance, 172
Liability, 180
LOGMARS, 181

M

Management Approach, 173
Marketing Partners Identification
    Number, 39-40
Master Solicitation Document, 101
Material Inspection and
    Receiving Report, 185
McNamara-O'Hara Service
    Contract Act, 171
Methods of searching, 51-54
Military Engineering Data Asset
    Locator System, 104
Military packaging, 144-145, 180
Minimum Acceptance Period, 157
Minimum wage, 155-156, 171
Minority Business Development
    Agency, 90

Minority-Owned Businesses, 77
Modifications, 50-51, 71-73
MPIN, 44
Multi-Agency Contracts, 27

N

NAFTA, 155, 199, 217
NAICS code, 53-54, 75, 126
National Acquisitions Center, 128
National Standards System
    Network, 125
National Stock Numbers (NSN),
    95, 100, 120, 123, 181
Natural disasters, 91-92
North American Industrial
    Classification System, 28, 41
Numbered Notes, 71

O

Offeror's Representations and
    Certifications Applications
    Worksheet, 199, 206-223
Online Representations and
    Certifications Application, 28,
    44-45
Opening date, 50
ORCA, 166, 206

P

PACE, 101, 116
Past Performance Information
    Retrieval System, 70, 191-192
Past Performance, 150, 160-162,
    166, 170, 174, 175, 191-192
Performance Work Statements, 74
Place of Manufacture Clause, 157
Post-Award Orientation
    Conference, 189
Price Proposal, 166

Procurement Automated Contract Evaluation program, 93, 98-99

Procurement Gateway (ProGate), 117-127

Procurement Technical Assistance Centers, 27, 31, 182

Product Accessibility Template, 91

Product Data Management Division, 124

Progress reports, 190

Public Key Infrastructure, 187

Purchase Cards, 28, 32

Q

Q-Quotes, 120

Q-Solicitation, 120

Qualified Manufacturers List, 80-81

Qualified Products List, 80

Quality Shelf Life Program, 94, 105-106

R

Radio Frequency Identification (RFID) tags, 181-182

S

Searching, methods of, 51-54

Section 508, 91

Secure File Transfer Protocol (SFTP), 188

Service contracts, 165-177

Service-Disabled Veteran-Owned Businesses, 77-78, 211

Set-aside programs, 48, 75-78

Shipping, 183

Site Visit, 73, 172

Size standards, 28-29

Small Business Act, 84-85

Small Business Administration (SBA), 27, 28, 75, 76, 131

Small Business Concern, 75

Small business, resources for, 29-31

Small Disadvantaged (8a) Businesses, 76, 211

Small Minority-Owned Businesses, 77

Social Security number, 37

Sole Source, 78-80

Solicitation Numbering System, 97-98

Solicitation Package, 74-75

Solicitation/Contract Form, 137-141

Standard Competition, 176

Standard Industrial Classification Codes, 42

Standard Inspection Requirement, 184

Standard Practice for Commercial Packaging, 179

Statement of Work, 74, 167-169

Stop-Work Order, 190

Streamlined Competition, 176-177

Sub-contracting opportunities, 131

Subcontracting, 156, 170

SUB-Net, 90, 131

Synopsis, understanding the, 59

T

Tax Identification number (TINS), 37-38, 209-210

Technical Approach, 173

Technical documents, 102-105

Technical Proposal, 166-169

T-Quotes, 120

Trade Agreements Certificate, 157

Trading Partners Identification Number, 38-39

T-Solicitation, 120

U

U.S. Patent Office, 130-131
U.S. Postal Service, 127
U.S. Trade Agreement, 199, 223-227
U.S./Canada Joint Certification Program, 102
UNICOR, 68, 129
Uniform Contract Format, 136-162
Unique Identification of Items, 181
Unit of Issue Codes, 143, 200, 228
USAGov, 90

V

Vendor Notification Service, 91
Vendor Self Service system, 131
Very Small Business Concern, 75
Veteran-Owned Businesses, 77-78, 208, 211
Veterans Administration, 128

Veterans reporting requirement, 192
VETS, 194
Virtual Data Center Services, 195

W

Wage determinations, 170-171
Walsh-Healey Public Contracts Act, 171
Web Invoicing System (WINS), 186
WebFlis, 100
Wide Area Work Flow (WAWF), 182, 186-189
Wide Area Work Flow Receiving Report, 184
Woman-Owned Business Concern, 76
Woman-Owned Business, 208-209, 211
Wood packaging material, 182
Workers compensation, 172

ABOUT

THE AUTHORS

ABOUT MALCOLM PARVEY

As an independent sales and marketing professional for 30 years, Mal specializes in helping small businesses sell their products and services to the federal government. Based in Franklin, Massachusetts, he works exclusively with small businesses, assisting them in every aspect of the government marketplace, from finding appropriate opportunities and locating drawings or specifications, to completing the paperwork and following up on the awards. He offers services to submit the General Services Administration's "GSA Schedule" proposal and the Department of Defense's "E-Mall" program, as well as his expertise in all aspects of the federal government marketplace.

"I started looking into this market in 1977. I read everything I could find, went to seminars, visited agencies, and spoke to anyone that would talk to me. At a time when computers weren't on everyone's desk, much of the work had to be done through the mail. Written requests for information about a pending bid opportunity could take as long as 10 days to receive! While holding down a full-time job and maintaining a wife and two kids it took me over two years to submit my first offer. After a few false starts, I put in an offer on behalf of a food broker to supply dairy products to five Veteran Administration hospitals, and we were awarded the contract! One reason for the success of this bid was that I was able to find out the current price of the contract through the Freedom of Information Act *before* we submitted our bid. A year later I had six clients and quit my job."

Mal has worked with many different small businesses, in many diverse markets since then, so that his experience is not limited to just one type of business, but rather spans a wide range of companies in the commercial marketplace.

Mal has published this training book that gives small businesses the opportunity to get involved in this marketplace. By taking a step-by-step approach, the book allows small businesses with no previous knowledge of this marketplace to begin selling to the federal government.

"Many small businesses wish to get involved in this market, but have no-one to help them get started. This book shows someone with no experience in this marketplace exactly where to begin."

About Deborah Alston

Deborah Alston was born in Great Britain, and attended the University of Wales in Swansea, where she obtained her Bachelor of Arts degree in English literature with honors. She has lived in the United States for more than 20 years. She has previously worked in the Information Department of a large biotechnology company, and has worked closely with Mr. Parvey for the last four years putting together this book. Deborah currently lives in Louisville, Kentucky, with her husband and two children.